Contents

Helicopters and North Sea Oil

Helicopters and North Sea Oil

A Story of Service, Danger and Survival

Peter Saxton

PEN & SWORD
HISTORY

First published in Great Britain in 2023 by
Pen & Sword History
An imprint of
Pen & Sword Books Ltd
Yorkshire – Philadelphia

Copyright © Peter Saxton 2023

ISBN 978 1 39906 037 0

A CIP catalogue record for this book is
available from the British Library.

Typeset by Mac Style
Printed in the UK by CPI Group (UK) Ltd, Croydon, CR0 4YY.

Pen & Sword Books Limited incorporates the imprints of Atlas,
Archaeology, Aviation, Discovery, Family History, Fiction, History,
Maritime, Military, Military Classics, Politics, Select, Transport, True
Crime, Air World, Frontline Publishing, Leo Cooper, Remember
When, Seaforth Publishing, The Praetorian Press, Wharncliffe Local
History, Wharncliffe Transport, Wharncliffe True Crime, White Owl
and After the Battle.

For a complete list of Pen & Sword titles please contact

PEN & SWORD BOOKS LIMITED
47 Church Street, Barnsley, South Yorkshire, S70 2AS, England
E-mail: enquiries@pen-and-sword.co.uk
Website: www.pen-and-sword.co.uk

Or

PEN AND SWORD BOOKS
1950 Lawrence Rd, Havertown, PA 19083, USA
E-mail: Uspen-and-sword@casematepublishers.com
Website: www.penandswordbooks.com

DEDICATED TO ALL WHO WORKED
ON THE NORTH SEA.

Acknowledgments

This book was the result of three things.

Firstly, a shared experience – what it was like to work on the North Sea, deploying one's chosen skills, thereby making an indispensable contribution to the safety and smooth running of a massive operation and to the economy of the United Kingdom.

Secondly, a sense amongst the participants that this is a story worth telling – to capture some of their experiences and to share them.

Thirdly, a willingness to sit down at a desk and give time writing when you could have been on the golf course.

I am grateful to the large number of colleagues who submitted scripts for consideration. It has been possible to include only some of them.

I am grateful to Captain Lou Demarco, the person who originally made the requests for contributions, and who himself provided a particularly significant chapter in this book. The book had often been talked about, but it was Lou's energy that got the ball rolling.

Finally, I must express especial gratitude to Carole, wife of the late Captain Campbell Bosanquet, the chief illustrator of the book. Campbell was a talented photographer and his work has achieved a special place in bringing the book to life. I am grateful to her for her generosity in making his pictures available.

Peter Saxton.

Preface

The provenance of this study of one of the impacts of the helicopter on modern aviation is long and varied.

I first met the commissioning author, Dr. Peter Saxton, when he was a student at University College Swansea, reading Politics and, more particularly, for a specialised third year undergraduate paper in Strategic Studies. I taught for many years both at Swansea and elsewhere in a 60 year career including two final decades in the Department of War Studies at King's College, London.

Barry Sheerman was a Lecturer in American Politics at the University College and subsequently was elected to become a successful and senior member of the House of Commons where he was Chairman of the Education Committee but also manifested an enduring concern with issues of air transport safety. He was, for example, instrumental in launching **PACTS**, the Parliamentary Advisory Council for Transport Safety.

Peter Saxton's early career was flying helicopters, military and civil, before moving on to senior airline management and academic research.

Peter Saxton and his colleagues have done well to contribute so effectively by providing first hand accounts of their involvement flying helicopters in the North Sea oil boom. I for one welcome such an impressive analysis, derived from a wide range of perspectives.

Finally, all three of us wish to thank Dr Lester Crook for his diligence in managing the publication processes to a successful conclusion. All of us hope that readers will find this volume both instructive and a pleasure to read.

J. E. Spence
Professor, Department of War Studies
King's College, London

Forword By Barry Sheerman

Member Of Parliament

Elected in 1979, I recall a colleague telling me, on my first day in Parliament, that Labour would not win an election for very many years as the Thatcher government would inherit the vast oil wealth about to be pumped out from the North Sea.

These were exciting times, from the first news that huge oil deposits had been discovered under UK waters, to the ensuing scramble to make the most of this oil bonanza. The serious challenges of extracting, pumping, and delivering this resource in such a hostile environment necessitated the development of cutting-edge technologies and unique human skills.

The story of how this battle was lead, organised and won deserves thoughtful and detailed analysis. Until now little has been written by the very people who brought their skills, courage, and determination to the unfolding North Sea Oil saga.

I had always had a keen interest in transport safety and very early in my parliamentary career I launched, with other colleagues, PACTS, the Parliamentary Advisory Council for Transport Safety.

Coincidentally, I also began a Parliamentary fellowship with BP soon after taking my seat and made several visits to remote oilrigs in some challenging weather conditions. It would be an understatement to say that what I witnessed had a profound and lasting influence on my understanding of the size, scale and challenges of oil exploration in such a hazardous environment.

At that time my former student, Peter Saxton, now a helicopter pilot had taken a key role, based in Aberdeen and servicing the oil rigs. Knowing of my interest in transport safety and the North Sea, he contacted me as he had serious concerns.

At the peak of the oil boom the transportation of men and materials by sea was proving difficult and dangerous and the use of helicopters was proving vital. The search for qualified pilots became frantic and it was pilots from the RAF, the Royal Navy, and the British Army that stepped up. The helicopter industry with its great engineering expertise played a key role in all this, but there was clear evidence that in the haste to get the oil up and out heightened risk levels were tolerated. As a consequence, the lives of divers, pilots and, passengers were put in peril. All this was relatively new territory for the Civil Aviation Authority, and it appeared, at times, to struggle with its North Sea Helicopter responsibilities.

Tragically the Piper Alpha disaster in 1988 was a global wakeup call to the oil drilling industry and the experience, testimony, and commentary of another of my Swansea students Ed Punchard, who was a diver on the stricken oil rig, is compelling reading (Piper Alpha: A survivor's story). This was a key insight into how the tragedy occurred.

There have been few serious attempts to put the North Sea Oil story into the context of the time, particularly from the viewpoint of someone seriously involved at the sharpest of sharp ends of this phenomenal adventure. We owe Peter Saxton and Jack Spence, a distinguished academic and one of my former university colleagues, a significant debt for this exciting, insightful work.

Chapter One

The Beginnings of the North Sea Oil Boom

Captain Peter Saxton

In the autumn of 1969, oil was discovered for the first time deep below the bed of the North Sea.

The excitement quickly became palpable, because the extent to which the UK was having to import oil from other countries to keep the economy going, especially from unstable areas such as the Middle East, rendered the country economically and strategically vulnerable.

The prospect of the UK becoming an oil producer and exporter seemed to be the answer to these important problems, a way out of Britain's corrosive boom-bust cycles, and of access to huge revenues enabling British governments to drive more ambitious political programs. It was also not lost on British politicians that what Prime Minister Harold Wilson called a "bonanza" offered not just the next General Election victory, but possibly a string of them.

Just when many were thinking that was as good as it could get, it got better – a lot better. In 1973 the Organisation of Oil Exporting Countries (OPEC), the Middle East oil cartel that fixed oil prices, quadrupled the price from $3 to $12 per barrel. Whatever everyone's projected revenue guesses had been, they had, at a stroke, increased four-fold.

The big oil companies began to arrive in Aberdeen, whose geographical position and infrastructure made it an obviously attractive operational base area. The northeast of Scotland also had a multitude of natural harbours such Aberdeen, Peterhead, the Moray Firth, Cromarty, the Orkney Isles including the huge harbour of Scapa Flow, and the Shetland Islands, from where to set up offshore re-supply bases. New yards were constructed from scratch. Drilling activity in the North Sea accelerated as part of the west's search for oil sources in stable areas of the world. The oil companies were international economic giants with two things that the west needed – the financial resources, and the technical clout to take on these new levels of challenge an order of magnitude more difficult than even they were used to. Their current technology was going to have to be developed further to cope.

The North Sea, especially in winter, can produce monstrous waves, and winds of storm and occasionally hurricane force. The structures required to achieve the oil extraction would have to be equally massive to withstand the battering; this degree of resilience and robustness was without precedent. Oil structures had already been destroyed by storms with loss of life during the exploration phase in the 1960s. Bigger, heavier ones were under construction by the mid 1970s, some weighing in the order of thirty thousand tonnes and reaching up to two hundred feet high above the waves. These were the production platforms, moved by sea and fixed to the seabed over the well-heads that had been discovered by the smaller floating drilling platforms. The largest was Chevron's Ninian Central Platform – the largest structure ever built in the United Kingdom so far. Built at Kishorn, when it was transported on its rafts from the west coast of Scotland it was claimed to have been the heaviest man-made object ever to move over the surface of the earth. It weighed over six hundred thousand tonnes.

In the race to be the first to get oil ashore, it looked like British Petroleum (BP) was on the home straight with the Forties Field. They were beaten, however, by a much smaller player – Hamilton Oil – who did so by the innovative expedient of dispensing with expensive and time-consuming construction of oil and gas pipe-lines to get the oil from the well-head to the shore. They constructed oil loading points, sometimes called "Spa's", from which to fill tankers to transport the oil to the coast. In late summer 1975 the first oil arrived at The Isle of Grain.

Despite weather, technical problems that would have been insurmountable in other industries, and lots of political shoulder-barging over taxation rates, Britain appeared to be on course for self-sufficiency in oil by 1980.

Impressive as the ability to assemble resources and develop technology undoubtably was, there were structural aspects of the way the oil industry decided to organise itself that could have been critical but for good fortune. It comprised largely outsourced arrangements, with oil company personnel taking the supervisory and command roles. Manning and supplying the operation were outsourced to contracting specialists. The saturation divers living on the sea-floor to service the submerged sections, the roustabouts on the drilling floor, the service staff in the accommodation modules, the ships and their companies that carried supplies out and back to port, and the helicopters and crews that supported them from the skies, were all services supplied by specialist companies.

This is a story about the helicopter crews. This book is written almost entirely by former North Sea helicopter pilots and crew members. It is part of their contribution to an epic enterprise that changes the fortunes of the United Kingdom for the better, albeit at a grave cost. The resulting economic transformation and its consequences would not have been possible had it not been for the serendipitous fact that highly experienced professional helicopter crews were already available to the industry and to the country. Initially they came mostly from the British armed services, but with some from the United States and other countries.

Sources: Wasted Windfall – TV documentary c.1994

Chapter Two

An Introduction to Helicopters

Captain Peter Saxton

Towards the end of the construction of this book, two of the learnéd scholars, who were part of the proof-reading group, Professor Jack Spence and Dr Lester Crook, pointed out to me that for many people helicopters are a mystery. This was emphasised by my wife Barbara a couple of days later when she asked innocently "Why are they called helicopters?"

I have flown thousands of hours in these machines, but I had to admit that I had never considered it before. So I looked it up.

The name is derived from two Greek words. "Heli" from "helix" or a screw-shaped coil; and "pteron" meaning "wing". Leonardo da Vinci produced drawings of such machines as early as the fifteenth century. They do not look aerodynamically viable, especially as it was assumed that manpower alone could get them airborne, but it shows that the possibility of vertical flight and presumably the uses to which it could be put was being considered hundreds of years ago.

The Concise Oxford Dictionary defines a helicopter as "a type of aircraft without wings, obtaining lift and propulsion from horizontally revolving overhead blades or rotors, and capable of moving vertically and horizontally".

I had learned to fly on De Havilland Chipmunks with the University Air Squadron. I joined the Royal Air Force and had graduated as a Pilot Officer from the Officer Cadet Training Unit at RAF Henlow. I was awarded the Sword of Honour.

We were then posted to RAF Church Fenton for a month of concentrated maths and physics to ready us for jet training at

RAF Leeming in North Yorkshire. Jet conversion was done on a superb little plane called the Jet Provost, which was the training version of the BAC Strikemaster, a light ground attack aircraft that had seen action in various theatres.

There were three versions, or marques, available. The Mk 3 was under-powered and consequently the most complicated to fly. It was irreverently referred to as "the constant thrust, variable noise machine". The Mk 4 had considerably more power and was a real treat. The Mk 5 had the tip tanks removed and so looked very slick. It also had a pressurised cockpit so it was quiet to fly and more comfortable at high altitudes. However, that pressurisation was at the expense of thrust. My favourite was the Mk4. I liked the extra power. Throughout my flying career I always craved extra power. The most powerful of the version was the Strikemaster to enable it to carry a war-load, but we didn't have any of those at Leeming. Pity.

So we spent a memorable year roaring around the north of England and low level over Wales having a grand time as we worked towards our "Wings". The day came eventually; we were awarded the coveted brevet and streaming for advanced flying training began.

This was probably the first important career decision for us to make, but there was a problem. It seems hard to credit now, but at that time the RAF actually had a glut of trainee pilots. In those days the RAF retained the same command structure as World War 2 had made famous – Fighter, Bomber, Coastal and Transport Commands; plus Training Command where we were now. There was also, de facto, a sixth joke "Command" which was referred to ironically as "Holding Command". This referred to those many spare pilots. It wasn't much of a joke, not if you happened to be a spare pilot, fully trained and raring to go. Time to be posted to an Operational Conversion Unit (OCU) could be measured in years. Some of them were diverted to Central Flying School at RAF Little Rissington to go straight from advanced flying training to instructor training and then at least one tour instructing as a Qualified Flying Instructor (QFI).

Without any squadron experience at all this was hardly ideal neither operationally nor in terms of morale. Life on a Squadron was what it was all about and instructing traditionally came later with a couple of operational tours behind you. Not anymore. Some took it well, grateful that at least it was a flying tour; they were referred to as "Creamed-off QFIs". These men had generally done well during their training and were picked for that reason, so it was a compliment really. However, quite a few refused to see it that way, were disgruntled with their lot and generally they showed it. For this reason they were referred to in the vernacular as "Creamed off, Pissed off QFIs".

In the RAF, squadrons used to have a senior Flight Lieutenant designated as Adjutant, and he often served as something of a mentor to more junior pilots, who referred to him as "Uncle". But then the RAF decided to do away with the position and that left – nothing. One assumes that the Flight Commanders were supposed to pick this up this responsibility, but if so it didn't work well, not in my experience anyway.

However, I did have one very important thing going for me personally – a real Uncle – my Mother's younger brother, Bernard Lax. He had run away to join the RAF as soon as he was old enough. Like so many others then he was breaking his neck to fly. Unfortunately, that was around 1939, a date to conjure with. He went on to fly four-engined Handley Page Halifaxes in Bomber Command, and Bristol Beaufighters on anti-shipping strikes in Coastal Command. He didn't talk about it much, but I learned later that he had been shot up twice and once ditched in a freezing cold Norwegian fjord. The RAF sent a De Havilland Mosquito from Scotland across the North Sea to bring him back. He flew home in the bomb bay. Back at base they gave him a medical, a week's leave and then he was straight back on operations. He was lucky to get through it. At the end of the war, he changed to the Technical Branch and became an electronic engineering officer at Wing Commander rank. He acted as my private mentor. He tutored me before I went for aircrew selection at RAF Biggin Hill. The applicants were referred to as "COBY" (Cream of Britain's Youth) and they imagined we didn't know.

We sat in Uncle's front room sipping cold beer while he quizzed me on my knowledge of Jaynes Aircraft, the RAF's command structure, principles of flight and anything else he thought appropriate.

"They will ask you to comment about the cancellation of the British Tactical Strike Reconnaissance Aircraft (TSR2) and the correct answer is that the cancellation is a disaster. This is the one time in the interview that you may show some emotion. Don't overdo it – mild exasperation is about right. They will ask you why. The correct answer is that it was designed specifically to meet the RAF's strategic and tactical needs. Any other choice will be a second choice. And personally, I think it was a world beater so we could have flogged them like hot cakes. I suspect for that reason the Americans didn't want it to succeed so you can make of that what you like but probably best to avoid getting drawn into it at the interview. Unless of course they ask, in which case you can let rip. They will ask you what you know about the American F-111 which looks like it's in contention as a replacement for the TSR2. It looks to me like an electronic nightmare frankly, but don't actually say that either. Don't use the expression "swing-wing" – it's too tabloid press – use the expression "variable geometry" which means the same thing but makes you sound like you know what you're talking about. Be that as it may I think you now know enough. This is an interview not an exam and they won't expect expertise just yet. Be serious but pleasant and if you don't know the answer to a question, say so – don't bluff".

Anyway, it worked and I was commissioned as a trainee officer.

At the end of basic flying jet course I was awarded my "Wings" and had further conversations with my Uncle.

"I suppose it goes without saying that you don't want to become an instructor yet?"

"No thanks Uncle – I want to get on a squadron."

"Yes, well everybody does Pete, that's pretty much the problem. How's your close- formation flying?"

"OK – enjoyed it – but they're not going to send me to the Red Arrows as a first tourist."

"No, I wasn't thinking about them. Have you considered helicopters? You have to be able to hover, that's what it's all about, and hovering is really just close formation on a bit of ground or a bit of a ship or a building and so on. It's one place we don't have enough pilots. They have a high failure rate on the conversion course".

"No I've not considered it".

"Well I urge you to and here are some reasons. Firstly, if you're lucky you could get an overseas posting as your first tour. Singapore, Hong Kong to name a few. Exotic places. Secondly, you can always transfer back to fixed-wing flying after one or two tours, but then you would have operational experience under your belt, and that's a big tick in the box. The Brass think helicopters are the coming thing. It's dawning on the powers that be that these machines are battle winners. Look what's happening in south-east Asia – the Americans would be in a right jam without them.

I'd stay away from Search and Rescue if you can though – I've heard that described as 95% boredom and 5% abject terror. Oh, one other thing. The Advanced Flying Training School is at RAF Tern Hill in Shropshire. I understand the chop-rate on the course is high – someone said around 60%. You'll have to concentrate. It's going to seem strange when you've been blatting about in jets".

I returned to RAF Leeming from a course break. We were given an option form on which we were told to state three preferences which might decide which advanced course we would undergo. I put the single word "Helicopter" in all three choices. One of the instructors, a former fighter pilot, used to refer to helicopters as "frantic palm-trees". He said

"Well you certainly seem to know what you want and I can see some method in it. Good luck with the 'frantics' then. Word to the wise, they do seem to have a high fail rate at Tern Hill. I can't say I'm surprised – they are very different".

"Yes Sir – I've been told".

I arrived at Central Flying School (Helicopters) at RAF Tern Hill in Shropshire, and with only about 250 hours of jet and piston fixed-wing experience, helicopters were indeed a mystery. I had little understanding of how they flew at all. The rotor at the top was understandable because I understood propellors and that's just a big propellor I told myself. But what did the one at the back do?

I started to compile a list of tasks that a helicopter might be expected to do which could not be undertaken by a fixed-wing aeroplane. The obvious difference was that a helicopter could rise vertically into the air. But then so could a Harrier "jump jet" so there was a certain amount of overlap around. Normally, a fixed wing aeroplane has to use a runway to propel itself above stalling speed before it can become airborne, and to manage the same state during an approach to a landing. So, the helicopter was an aircraft that was designed not to stall at low airspeed, even when this was zero, or indeed the aircraft was flying backwards. Neat.

Then came the full appreciation that the aircraft was a platform – but one that could stand still in the air. I had experienced this in flying training. As trainee pilots we were taken out from Bridlington in a RAF Rescue Launch and invited to step off the stern into the North Sea. This was the position we would find ourselves in if we ever had to bail out or eject from an aircraft. The ejection sequence was automatic so in that particular event we didn't have much to do until, dangling from the parachute, we descended into the sea. At that point we had to get cracking with drills.

After inflating the life jacket and the individual dinghy we climbed in, put up the roof, bailed out the water and inspected the contents of the personal survival pack (PSP). We were, of course, waiting for the launch to pick us up again, or better still for the search and rescue (SAR) helicopter to arrive. We heard him coming, broke out flares, flashed heliographs, waved, and climbed on top of the collapsed dinghy roof. The helicopter from RAF Leconfield was a Westland Whirlwind based on the Sikorsky S55 but with a Rolls-Royce Gnome turboshaft engine. It clattered into the overhead and the downdraft hit us. As it approached a Winchman swung outside the aircraft and the Winch Operator lowered him towards us. It was impressive to see how fast that team worked. The pilot was conned over the dinghies by the Winch Operator talking on the intercom "......Forward one....... Steady steady..........Good hover". The pilot of course could now not see the dinghy nor the survivor, nor his Winchman working below. He flew it manually as there was no automatic hovering equipment such as the Navy used for their extended hovering pinging for submarines. We were briefed to sit still on the dinghy and not attempt to assist the Winchman. Let him do it all – you would just make his job more difficult if you tried to be clever. He almost threw the padded strop over your head, underneath your armpits, tightened the toggle and gave a thumbs up but kept clasping you with his other arm. There was a slight jerk and the two of us started to rise up away from the dinghy as the winch wire was wound in by the winch.

Then came the finessing bit. The helicopter had taken up the hover just high enough to keep the lashing sea-spray whipped up by the rotor out of the engine intake. You didn't want salt spray entering your engine; but you didn't want the two people on the wire to be pulled up to a big height in case one of them fell off, or it was necessary to guillotine the wire in an emergency. So, the helicopter was moved forward fast enough to leave the spray behind and descended at the same rate as the winch was bringing in the wire. This kept the crewman and survivor just above the water so that no injury was possible. It looked as if the helicopter was lowering itself down its own wire, which, in a sense it was.

"Crewman and survivor at the door............crewman and survivor inside and strapping in.......you are clear behind..........door coming closed......clear up and away!"

The Whirlwind picked up speed, turned towards the coast and had this been the real thing and not a practice would fly as fast as possible towards Bridlington Hospital or RAF Leconfield Medical Centre. He would use the callsign "Playmate", which told the Air Traffic unit that he was a SAR helicopter on a rescue, and the sky would be cleared for him inbound. A medical team with an ambulance would already be waiting at the helipad.

Sometimes it can be very quick. In 1973, a Westland Wessex helicopter manned by the elite SD (Special Duties) crew from RAF Odiham in Hampshire, was winch-training on the south coast when the crew of three picked up a Mayday call from an RAF Harrier. The aircraft's single Pegasus engine had failed and Harriers had a reputation for gliding like a brick. The pilot gave a position report that almost coincided with the Wessex's position and ejected from the aircraft. The crew turned the Wessex, and sure enough, there he was, floating down under his parachute. The Harrier hit the water and sank. The SD Wessex was almost on top of the pilot as he entered the water with the Winchman on his way down on the wire. It must have been the fastest rescue on record between independently operating aircraft.

What was it in the technical and engineering history of rotorcraft development that enabled the sort of operations described above and throughout this book? The history of rotorcraft development is longer than might be thought. The helicopter was preceded by the Autogiro, developed around 1920 by Juan de la Cierva. The rotor was not powered but free spinning and backward tilting. When the propellor pulled the aircraft forward the airflow through the rotor spun it, developing the lift required. The unpowered rotor could not provide a vertical take-off or landing (VTOL), but it could achieve very high angles of take-off and approach-to-landing which were close to vertical (STOL or Short take-off and landing.) It was not able to hover or fly backwards in still air.

The first fully controllable helicopter was developed in Germany by the Focke-Achgelis Company. It had characteristics of both the autogiro and the helicopter. It had the aero-engine driven propellor of an autogiro combined with engine-driven twin rotors of the helicopter mounted on pylons on either side of the fuselage. It was stable yet agile, two characteristics that are not easily rendered compatible. This aircraft gained fame when test pilot Hanna Reitsch demonstrated its manoeuvrability by flying it in front of a huge crowd *inside* the Deutschlandhalle in Berlin in 1938.

These early models were essentially experimental, but the first production helicopter was the Sikorsky R-4. Named Hoverfly, it was trialled by the US Army in 1942, who were so impressed with it they placed an order for 100 machines. These were used in the Second World War, only on the Allied side, for transport and reconnaissance.

Igor Sikorsky did not have the field to himself. Frank Piasecki experimented with twin tandem rotor machines during the 1940s. The original piston-engine machines were limited on power, but improved versions incorporating gas turbine engines flew in 1955. Sadly, the contract for production of these machines was cancelled. They are often regarded as a precursor to the CH47 Chinook.

A new and interesting development also appeared in the 1950s, called the Rotodyne.

Built by the British company Fairey, it was a triple hybrid, part autogyro, part helicopter and part aeroplane. It had fixed wings which mounted two turbo-prop engines. The rotor was free-spinning in forward flight and the lift generated supported half the aircraft's weight, the wings the other half. To achieve vertical take-off and landing (VTOL) the engines provided high pressure gas into the rotor blades, which was expelled through tip-jets, which drove the rotors around under power, at which point it was flying as a helicopter. This system did not utilise torque however, so it required no tail rotor, saving power. As the aircraft transitioned to forward flight, pressure to the tip jets was reduced until it became a free-spinning rotor again. It developed into a viable airliner able to carry up to 40 passengers. The VTOL capability of a helicopter could be combined with the efficiency of a fixed wing cruise, and it promised to revolutionise inter-city flight economics.

It was not to be. The tip jets were infernally noisy, and concerns arose about adverse reactions to such high noise levels from the populations of cities, which were echoed in the Concorde project 20 years later. The Rotodyne was also reliant on government funding.

The British aeroplane building industry was deeply and inefficiently fragmented, so the government forced mergers and groupings to take place. As a result of all this turmoil there were casualties and project cancellations, and the Fairey Rotodyne was one such.

In the military field, a number of viable helicopters emerged in the late 1940s. The Korean War 1950-3 was the first war that included the widespread use of helicopters by a western power. The popularity of the film "MASH" (Mobile Army Surgical Hospital) released in 1970, and the long-running T.V. series that aired from 1972 to 1983 featuring the antics of Hawkeye, Radar, Spear-chucker and Nurse "Hot-Lips" Houlihan, ensured that the Bell 47 included in the opening sequences became instantly recognisable to millions of viewers.

The speed of getting a wounded soldier off the battlefield and under medical supervision was critical to saving life but the helicopter's usefulness did not end at casualty evacuation. They were also used for reconnaissance as was the Hoverfly in WW2, artillery spotting, combat rescue of pilots downed behind enemy lines, as well as general transport. One enterprising pilot even managed to fix forward-firing machine guns to the Bell 47, and fire them in the hover by tugging on cords attached to the triggers. Given that a helicopter pilot maintaining a hover has both hands full it must remain a matter of conjecture as to exactly how he managed to do this. They were not used offensively. It did forecast things to come however – the armed attack helicopter or "gunship".

The Vietnam War, originating after WW2, was the prolonged conflict that brought the helicopter fully into fame. Night after night, TV news channels in the USA and in fact over the world followed the progress of the fighting and the political machinations. These reports often featured one helicopter more than any other – the Bell Iroquois – nicknamed the "Huey" after its US military designator, the HU-1 (Helicopter Utility 1). Based on Joseph Conrad's novel "Heart of Darkness", Francis Ford Coppola's film "Apocalypse Now" thrust unforgettable images of this machine further into the public consciousness and memory.

Based on the HU-I, Bell also came up with the first widely produced "gunship". With a drastically slimmed down fuselage this was a two place-machine, the weapons operator or gunner in the front cockpit, the pilot in the rear. Designated the Bell AH-1 (Attack Helicopter-1) "Cobra" it had a lot of parts in common with the Iroquois, an impressively cost-effective way to produce a two-seat gunship option, lightly armoured but heavily armed. They were called "Bushrangers". They flew gun escort to troop carriers, or individually as ground attack close support aircraft.

Other significant developments were taking place. Boeing-Vertol reintroduced the tandem rotor configuration in the forms of the CH (Cargo Helicopter) 46 Sea Knight and then the CH47 Chinook as a heavy lifter. The Sikorsky CH53 Sea Stallions provided heavy assault capabilities for the US Marines and Sikorsky CH54 Skycranes were optimised for picking up large or containerised loads or for under-slinging them.

Helicopter development was by no means exclusively carried out by the West. The former USSR had to exploit vast remote areas and the utility of the helicopter in doing so was obvious. They produced large numbers of robust workhorses, some of them of mind-boggling size. The largest rotorcraft ever produced was the Mil V-12 reputed to capable of lifting up to forty-four tonnes and transporting Inter-Continental Ballistic Missiles (ICBM).

This behemoth quickly became obsolete due technological advances but remains an astonishing tour de force and record-holder.

More practical and produced in numbers was the Mil 26. This was not in the same size-league as the MV-12, but still massive and drew crowds at air shows.

The Bell 47 Sioux was the first helicopter I learned to fly. With it's teetering head that produced a pronounced nod, there was, as had been predicted, little comparable with anything I had experienced before. It was piston engined, turbo-charged, the cockpit was a

Perspex bubble, the fuselage was a cage of struts only, and it had skids not wheels. To say you felt exposed is to put it lightly. The second part of the course involved a conversion on to the Westland Whirlwind, which turned out to be the aircraft I would fly on the first half of my first squadron tour in Singapore and Malaysia learning to support jungle troops from Australia, New Zealand and the UK (the ANZUK force).

The second half of the tour was spent flying the Wessex HC2 in and out of jungle clearings doing the same short range transport task, but this time with a helicopter that had two turbo-shaft engines, a lot more power, and some decent automatics for blind flying in cloud. This was more like it. I remained on the Wessex for the remainder of my time in the RAF, including a tour on special operations.

It would be true to say therefore that the period between the Second World War and the 1970s was the time that witnessed the rise to prominence of the helicopter. The standard of a horizontal main rotor combined with a vertical anti-torque tail rotor became the most common configuration by far with notable exceptions such as the Chinook. Research and development continued however in search of the Holy Grail – a hybrid that could combine the VTOL capability of a helicopter with the forward speed and range of a fixed wing turbo-prop aeroplane, something the Fairey Rotodyne had come so close to achieving in the 1950s. This was met with little success although many attempts were made such as tilt wing, tilt rotor, Advancing Blade Concept (ABC) and other ideas.

Eventually however, Bell Boeing enjoyed a break-through with the tilt rotor concept, which it developed through its JVX prototype and culminated in the tilt rotor V22 Osprey.

After years of testing and development it was ready to enter service in 1989 and is now in use with the US armed forces. The side-by-side rotors, mounted on the ends of a high wing, are rotated to the horizontal plane to give it a helicopter's VTOL capability. As the machine transitions to forward flight the rotors are rotated forward to the vertical plane becoming, in effect, a pair of huge propellors, conferring the range and forward speed of a turbo-prop aeroplane. A STOL capability is available to maximise fuel and payload, with the aircraft taking off and landing from a runway with the rotors in an intermediate position.

Squaring this circle at long last is an important achievement. Rotorcraft in their various forms were developed over the last hundred years, almost as long as the development of fixed wing aeroplanes. Throughout those parallel journeys it was mostly a choice – to do what an aeroplane can do in terms of speed and range; or to do what a helicopter can do in terms of VSTOL and prolonged hovering. In a sense, the combining of both in one practically viable aircraft is a coming of age that has been a long time coming.

As has been already noted, helicopters are particularly valuable, even essential, where there is a need to operate over remote or hostile regions. The North Sea qualifies as both.

Chapter Three

How Do They Do What They Do?

Captain Peter Saxton

A helicopter is a rotorcraft. There are many variations within this generic title, but by far the most numerous has always been the familiar 'chopper' configured with a large rotor above it to lift it from the ground, fly it forwards, backwards and sideways, and lower it back onto the ground again.

The helicopter was designed primarily to achieve this ability to carry out vertical take-off and landing (VTOL). Unlike a fixed wing aeroplane, its wings (rotor blades) do not stall when the aircraft slows down and even stops and flies backwards in mid-air provided the helicopter remains within its flight envelope. And unlike many other VTOL aircraft, it can sustain hovering flight for long periods of time.

The vertical take-off is achieved by increasing the lift developed by the rotor on all blades equally, and the pilot does this by pulling up a 'collective lever' which is held in the left hand.

Easy. So, what's all the fuss about?

Well, it's all about consequences, and there appears to be a lot of them to deal with when you first start learning to fly a helicopter, usually on a basic model. A basic fixed-wing aeroplane handles simply by comparison.

Those who studied physics at school will remember Newton's Laws of Motion, one of which is sometimes referred to as The Law of Action and Reaction. For every action there is an equal and opposite reaction. As the pilot pulls up the collective lever, it increases the pitch on all the rotor-blades equally. This increases the mass of the airflow being impelled downwards, which produces an equal and opposite force, an upward force called 'lift'. Eventually this force will equal the weight of the helicopter (another force), and the aircraft will go light on its wheels or skids. With further increase in collective pitch the lift force will over-come the weight force and the helicopter will accelerate upwards into a vertical climb.

At the same time as this is happening the rotor's speed is decaying because increasing lift increases rotor 'drag' a force which will slow down the rotor's speed. This is well demonstrated by trying to whisk a sheet of cardboard through the air. If the cardboard is edge-on to the direction of travel, the resistance is low; but if the cardboard is turned so it is flat to the direction of travel, the resistance, or drag, will be readily felt.

The rotor is designed to operate within a narrow band of rotational velocity expressed in revolutions per minute (RPM, or in the jargon 'revs'). The pilot must anticipate this decay in revs. and will counteract it by increasing engine power. In a basic model this is achieved by turning a twist-grip throttle mounted on the end of the collective lever, so the pilot's attention will be glued to the RPM gauge to ensure the revs remain within the prescribed limits. The pilot, (let's refer to as 'P' to avoid any gender difficulties) now has two vital controls in the left hand alone.

The helicopter is now free from the ground, which is where P. discovers that ground contact was actually preventing the aircraft from twisting laterally (yawing). Free of the ground, it will continue to yaw until P applies counteracting rudder to stop it. Failure to do this could result in disaster, so that's two things that could have gone badly wrong in the first few seconds. The power applied to the rotor to make the helicopter fly is delivered from the engine to the rotor by a series of rotating shafts. This twisting power is, of course, called 'torque' and at the point where it is delivered to the rotor, Newton's Law of Action and Reaction ('for every action there is an equal and opposite reaction') makes itself felt. The helicopter fuselage starts to rotate in the opposite direction to the rotor.

In a fixed wing aeroplane, the rudder is attached to the tail fin, which is ineffective until it has forward speed and therefore an airflow over it. However, the helicopter is now standing still in the air, with no airflow over its tail fin, which is therefore ineffective in providing directional stability, or in other words stopping the torque-induced yaw. This is what the tail rotor is for. Also driven by engine power through a series of shafts and gear- boxes, it acts in the same way as the main rotor except that it is vertically mounted and therefore provides a lateral thrust sideways instead of a vertical one downwards. The rudder-bar is therefore the same as a collective lever for the tail rotor. P applies rudder and brings the yaw under control. P now has the left hand, and both feet fully involved, with only the right hand empty. Any-thing else?

You bet. The helicopter has the ability to pitch and roll and drift off-spot in any direction. This could be due to wind, or horizontal drift caused by tail rotor thrust itself, but importantly to the fact that basic helicopters are unstable in all dimensions except yaw in forward flight. But P has dealt with yaw, so how does one correct for pitch and roll movements away from a level hover? In the right hand is a control column sometimes called a 'joy-stick'. In a helicopter it is called a cyclic stick. To control pitch (nose up or down) the cyclic is moved fore or aft. To control roll the cyclic is moved left or right. Like the collective and the rudder, this control is set up to be intuitive – if the helicopter pitches nose up the cyclic is moved forward to counteract and regain a level attitude – and so on.

Cyclic, collective and rudder movements must be co-ordinated with each other through most phases of flight.

Half of my first squadron tour in the Royal Air Force was spent in the Far East operating machines that were not much different from those described above. With practice, we became competent at it to the point that we could cope without too much thinking about it, but still they were a distraction and could demand attention in the wrong place at critical points in a flight, such as the onset of bad weather where navigation suddenly becomes a challenge. Low level flying demands maximum attention on position fixing and scrutinising the terrain ahead. In mountainous terrain there is often strong wind producing updrafts, downdrafts and turbulence that can be alarming; it can become a struggle to control the helicopter, so you need a machine capable of supporting you in your task. Flying without stabilisation aids and automation increases cockpit workload too, contributing to tiredness and fatigue. These are all flight safety issues.

To put this in perspective, it had been recognised that to expect handling pilots to deal with those sorts of variables in the course of normal sorties was not ideal. The good news was that by the early 1970s we were already in a transition phase. The RAF was re-equipping its squadrons with the Westland Wessex and the Aerospatiale Puma. The Royal Navy got the Westland-built Sea King based on a Sikorsky design.

These machines were brilliant by comparison. They boasted two powerful close-coupled gas turbine engines giving twin-engine safety and impressive power-weight capability. They were equipped with electronic flying stability, basic auto-pilots, cyclic stick stabilisation and feel. The control arrangements helped the pilot coordinate collective movements with rudder. Importantly, the engines, through a connected fuel control system, responded to collective movements and changed their power outputs automatically to match power demands to maintain rotor RPM within the tight required parameters. It was the development and incorporation of these innovations that made the difference. Not that we stopped practicing the raw flying – quite the reverse – continuation training tended to concentrate on it. And the reason is that any artificial aid to flying can go wrong, at which point you are back to basics. You always had to be able to revert to the raw basics when things went wrong.

But – for the North Sea we also needed machines that were impervious to icing, equipped with reliable area navigation systems, an instrument flying capability, and reliability of transmission systems. We still had a way to go.

Why were helicopter operations important during the North Sea Oil boom? This might seem like an obvious question but having engaged a number of people during the writing of this book I discovered that those who know about the North Sea oil boom at all (and some don't) will generally say that helicopters ferried the rig crews to and from the rigs. Most days it was A to B with a short take-off and landing (STOL) at base; plus the all-Important VTOL landing and take-off at the offshore installation or vessel. They provided transfers of people ship to ship, ship to offshore installation, and between installations. In marine pilot to ship transfers, these involved winching people on and off decks in all permissible conditions of day and night, sometimes involving high-line techniques, which are described elsewhere.

So far so good, and that was the big part of it, but it was by no means all. Helicopters provided search and rescue (SAR) services to the industry, which saved many lives.

They provided life-saving medical evacuation (MEDIVAC) services, getting life-threatened patients off ships and installations, sometimes at extreme range and in difficult weather, back to hospital in minimum time. Cases of rescuing saturation divers who had been taken ill on the sea-bed are also described elsewhere.

Alas, they also brought home the limits of even helicopters to alleviate catastrophe. As a young helicopter pilot, I believed the snatching from the jaws of death illusion. Until one dark night I was confronted with reality.

Chapter Four

The Development of Helicopter Operational Capabilities

Captain Tom Porteous

I joined British Airways Helicopters Ltd (BAHL) in August 1975. My course colleagues, ex-military and some fixed wing pilot re-treads, completed the ground school which was located in a portacabin outside the company building at Aberdeen Airport.

After ground-school exams, we commenced conversion to the S61N helicopter. The Training Captain assigned to complete this training was a former colleague from the days when we were both on fighters in the RAF.

Because of our flying experience, my intake progressed rapidly to First Officer after 3 months, and then we became Captains at the end of another three months. We were lucky that we joined in August, because one of the requirements to become a Captain was that you had to have flown through a North Sea winter as a co-pilot. There was a lot of severe weather over the North Sea, and I recall several times having to back on to a helipad because the wind was too strong for us to go in crosswind. The most memorable time was in a blizzard. That made for some interesting flying, backwards on to a deck, no crewman to talk us in (as in the RAF) and fighting the spatial orientation sensations of apparently flying forwards, (the snow whipping past us) whilst actually flying backwards.

Before I joined BAHL, the offshore installations in the northern part of the North Sea were not numerous, and so only a few rig crew rotations were required per week. The helicopters were deployed from Aberdeen to Shetland, and the crews spent a few days per month manning them. The pilots and engineers hadn't much to amuse themselves with up there, and one day they found a kilt washed up on the beach. They had it washed and dried, ready for use. There was a daily BA Viscount fixed wing service, and passengers walked from a portacabin check-in to the aircraft steps before being ushered into the aircraft. One of our pilots rolled his trouser legs up and put the kilt on. The kilt was slightly long for him. He wore his flying boots, and his BA Captain's jacket, complete with four gold rings on each arm. As the passengers began to walk across the tarmac, he marched swiftly to the front of them and lead them to the aircraft steps, saluting smartly as they climbed into the aircraft. He heard the pilot's window slide open, and a very cultured English voice said in his direction, "I don't know who you are or what you think you're doing, but f**k off!" No couth, or sense of humour, some people.

On another occasion when I was in "management", I had not flown enough over a period to retain my clearances to fly passengers. This required a check ride without passengers. On this particular day, there was no commercial flying because all the rigs were in thick fog. So it was decided that my check ride would go ahead. I had to do only one sector i.e., fly out to the rig, to regain my clearance. There was not even the need for me to land on the deck, because my landing currency was OK. So, the training captain and I set off in thick fog for one of the nearest rigs, still about an hour's flying away. Although I didn't need to actually land on the rig, I had to make an instrument approach to it. We got overhead and followed the procedure. We made contact with the sea surface at about 200ft but could not see the rig because of the poor visibility. However, we had radar, we could tell where the rig was, so we crept in towards it, and eventually made visual contact with the installation's legs sticking into the sea out of the gloom. The training captain said something like, it seems a pity to have come all this way and not get a cup of coffee and a sandwich. So we came to a hover with the rig's legs barely in sight, and wound up the altitude hold on our Automatic Flight Control System (AFCS) until we were level with the deck. It was easy then to slide across and land. This brought much jubilation to the rig crew who were ready to return to shore, although we had no replacements for them. Because I had fulfilled the requirements, I was now qualified to carry passengers again, so we had our coffees and brought the waiting crew home. We were the only helicopter to carry passengers that day, and as I was leaving our offices that evening with the Flight Operations Manager, he jokingly said that I had put a spanner in the works by being the only helicopter to bring a crew ashore, "You are a pimple on the a*se of progress," he continued. At which point one of the 'Bears' (oil rig worker) who was waiting for his taxi, got up, approached the Flight Operations Manager, and threatened to punch his lights out for speaking to "his" pilot like that!

In early 1976 I had become a Captain, and after a couple of years was appointed Flight Technical Officer (FTO). This job was expanded when the company bought more helicopter types and expanded further when the Civil Aviation Authority (CAA) required a Chief Test Pilot to be appointed because the Company held a Design Authorisation. The original appointment was to provide the link between the pilots and the engineering department. When the engineers wanted to make modifications to the aircraft, the pilots had a say in how it was introduced. At the beginning, British Airways Helicopters had only two types of helicopter, the Sikorsky S61 and the Sikorsky S58, both American designs. (There was also a single Jet Ranger, but that was considered by the Managing Director, Jock Cameron, to be his personal aircraft). They had only two of the S58s, and soon got rid of them when they were no longer commercially viable. Part of my responsibilities was to check out S61s which needed annual check flights, and also to test fly aircraft which had been in heavy maintenance at our engineering base to the south of the main airfield at Gatwick. We had a good size field in front of the Engineering hangar, and it was from there that I did most of the testing with the S61s. Jock Cameron retained his office in the Beehive, the old Air Traffic and Passenger Terminal at Gatwick. It was his habit, on Friday evenings after work to invite a bunch of the administrative staff to join him for a dram. He was from the North of Scotland, and invariably he had Glenmorangie on offer. When I was in Gatwick for weekend testing, he would include me in his party. It was here that I learned the correct pronunciation of the whisky from Tain with equal accent on each syllable.

Whenever an S61 was due its end-of-maintenance test flying, the engineers would call me down from Aberdeen to be ready when they finished the maintenance checks. It was amazing how many times I was called down on a Thursday but didn't get my hands on the aircraft until the Saturday morning. Nothing at all to do with the overtime payments made to engineers for working the weekend, of course. If all went well on the test flights, I would be sent on my way north to Aberdeen on the Sunday, usually late. Aberdeen Airport closed at about 10pm, and on quite a few occasions I could not get home in one go and had to night -stop at Newcastle. Quite a good banter was entered into between the Senior Ops Officer and my wife when he called to tell her I was stuck, yet again, in the Newcastle Airport Hotel. It was not a very high-class hotel, and I remember once having a drink in the bar, which had a pool table and gaming machines in it, when the barman ordered out a customer who appeared in his motorcycle helmet and leathers. The reason given was "You can't come into a lounge bar dressed like that!"

There still was a lot of technical development of the S61. One of my FTO tasks was to visit the Sikorsky factory to check that newly bought aircraft met our technical specifications along with a senior engineer who accepted the aircraft on our Company's behalf. I checked out the last two S61s that BAHL bought, and the aircraft which would fly the Airlink Service between Gatwick and Heathrow. When these aircraft had been accepted by the Company, they were stuck on a ship and transported across the Atlantic. When they arrived in Southampton Docks, they were met by a team of BAHL engineers who put the rotor blades back on, checked all systems seemed to work, and the FTO would start the aircraft up and fly to Gatwick Engineering Base. We always hoped everything would work first time, because the dockers told us that if we weren't off the dock by the time the next ship was due, we would be pushed over the side!

I collected two BAHL S61s from Southampton Docks, and the Airlink S61 from Le Havre. Airlink was made up of BAHL pilots and engineers, but the hostesses were from British Caledonian Helicopters. This company was set up to fly passengers between Gatwick and Heathrow Airports.

Sea Anchor Modification

The S61N was designed as an amphibian, and it was believed that, in the event of an engines and rotors shut down on water, the torque generated would cause the helicopter to roll over. Therefore, a sea anchor was provided which was designed to hold the aircraft against the torque during water shutdowns and keep the aircraft upright. The sea anchor pack looked a bit like a small parachute pack and was held either in a box on the bulkhead behind the co-pilot's head, or under the co-pilot's seat. To launch it, the co-pilot retrieved the sea anchor from its container, slid open or jettisoned the window to his left, reached out to retrieve a cord and clip which was retained under the outside of the window which, in turn, was secured to the front of the aircraft, clip the cord on to the rip-chord on the anchor, and throw the anchor out into the sea. It was expected that the fall from the window would cause a retaining pin to be withdrawn from the pack, and the anchor, which resembled a small parachute, would be released and fill with water under the surface. The rather complicated system was put to the test one night on the North Sea.

This ditching involved two senior management pilots. An emergency had been declared offshore one night, and an urgent bit of kit had to be taken to a rig. No passengers were needed and the two management pilots volunteered to carry out this operation. On the return flight, they experienced an emergency which caused them to land on the water. The sea was calm and there was little wind. It was decided that the engines and rotors needed to be shut down, so the captain ordered that the sea anchor be launched. The co-pilot did every action he was required to do, except attach the sea anchor to the chord before he threw the anchor out of the window. The sea anchor sank, but the subsequent shut down was completed very gingerly, and the helicopter remained upright. However, they were lucky, and had there been a heavy sea running their main rotor could have caught a wave, and the aircraft would have overturned.

It was decided that safety improvements were needed. The S61N originally had only one life raft for deployment in the event of a ditching. Also, the sponsons were expected to hold the aircraft upright whilst on the water. However, after experiencing several ditchings, it was decided to augment the buoyancy of the aircraft with inflatable "balloons" carried in the sponsons. A second life-raft was fitted to the rear emergency door, and a modification was introduced to enable the sea anchor to be launched more easily than the then-present situation.

This modification took the form of a housing outside and beneath the co-pilot's window, held in place by a lid which was spring loaded to hold it tightly in place. The sea anchor was permanently attached to its chord, and it was released by a two-movement action by the co-pilot, i.e. holding down a retaining latch and pulling the release handle. There was concern in the pilot ranks that, should the sea anchor be inadvertently deployed in flight, it would cause a catastrophic accident. So, we tested the release mechanism in flight, without the sea anchor being attached to the aircraft, and we could not get a combination of conditions in any permitted airspeeds or attitudes where the sea anchor could be deployed by the use of only one of the release mechanisms. We were completely satisfied of the safety of the modification, and to my knowledge, there has been no incident of inadvertent deployment.

Now we had to test the sea anchor's deploy ability in the water. The S61 has a large cargo door on the forward starboard side of the aircraft through which we would retrieve the soaking sea anchor. We had to be able to deflate the sea anchor after the deployment test, as we would not be able to lift the anchor when it was full of water. So, the design engineer arranged a deflation rope, which, when pulled by him in the back of the aircraft, would turn the parachute inside out, and he would be able to drag the anchor into the helicopter. Ever conscious of the safety aspects of any testing, we decided that we would fly to Shoreham, on the south coast of England, connect the test items whilst on the ground, and use the River Adur, right alongside the airfield, for out tests. We chose a Sunday to do this. Just in case we had difficulty in retrieving the sea anchor, we arranged with the Royal National Lifeboat Institute (RNLI) to have one of their inshore lifeboats available so that we could call it in and the lifeboat man could cut the sea anchor retaining rope to let us lift the helicopter off the water and land back at Shoreham.

When everything was ready, we started up and lifted over the airfield hedge on to the Adur. Sea anchor launch went perfectly, and it was interesting to see the large parachute-like device fill with water and settle under the surface. The design engineer, co-pilot and test pilot declared themselves satisfied with the modification. Then came the difficult part, deflation. The engineer pulled and pulled but could not deflate the sea anchor. Eventually, we called air traffic, and asked them to telephone the RNLI man. They called back to say he had been informed. However, of him there was no sign. We waited and eventually got fed up, and the co-pilot got out his survival knife, jettisoned his window (retrieving it into the cockpit), and he tried to reach the anchor's retaining rope, but it was too far out of his reach. He even stuck the upper part of his body out of the window, with the engineer holding on to his ankles, but he still couldn't reach. We were casting around wondering what to do next, when the engineer made a final attempt at deflating the anchor – and succeeded! He pulled the sea anchor into the aircraft, and we hopped back over the hedge onto the airfield and shut down to make everything safe again. Whilst we were getting everything back to normal for our short flight back to Gatwick, a small crowd had gathered to watch. In the crowd I noticed a chap with a large seaman's sweater with the initials "RNLI" across his chest. I enquired if he might be the inshore lifeboat man on duty to help us if we were in need. He said he was, and when I asked why he hadn't come to our rescue, he said, "Well, I could see you from the pub, and as you didn't seem to be in any great danger, I thought I'd finish my pint before coming to help."

No more donations to the RNLI from this test crew.

About a month later, we returned to Shoreham, and did a deployment test on the open sea. This time everything, including the deflation and recovery system worked as advertised. We did not require the RNLI.

Exporting Expertise – Developing an Operation from Scratch

BAHL won a contract to provide a couple of S61s to China for oil support in the South China Sea. The contest to win the contract was bitterly fought between BAHL and Bristow Helicopters.

Alan Bristow was a real fighter, and a savvy businessman. Negotiations between the Chinese and our two companies had been going on for a while, and the Chinese delegation, numbering several people, attended the Paris Air Show. I was at the Show, had seen the Chinese, and was able to call my boss in Aberdeen when I knew when they would land in Aberdeen. BAHL had arranged the visit, but Bristow arranged to meet the Chinese delegation, in order to whisk them away in limousines, whereas BAHL had arranged only a luxury coach. BAHL organised a reception for them in the Executive Club Lounge at Aberdeen Airport, and managed to bypass Bristow's reception committee.

The initial part of the plan was for us to train several Chinese helicopter pilots to fly the S61. These aircraft were to remain on the UK register, but were to be 'Chinese-ised'. Although the Chinese would fly them, they had to obey the UK CAA's requirements. The Chinese pilots, about half a dozen, had to go through the BAHL ground-school, pass the exams, and have their Chinese licences endorsed by the UK CAA. None of them spoke any English, and they arrived with a lady interpreter. The ground-school instructor never knew, when he asked questions at the end of each lesson, whether the answers were the student's or the interpreter's, although he thought it was the latter.

After having their licences endorsed, we started to teach them to fly the S61. Fortunately, they all were already helicopter pilots, and so it really was just a conversion exercise. Most of the flying training was done in our simulator, with the lady interpreter sitting in the jump seat. Their instructor, an ex-RAF helicopter instructor, did a super job, explaining each exercise to the students, flying it with them in the simulator, and later in the helicopter. I remember his frustration at their lack of English, because some of his instructions depended on their immediate understanding of what he was telling them and their correct reaction to his instructions. He took great trouble to explain that when he wanted to take control from the student, he would say, "I have control." The correct reaction was for the student to say, "You have control" and they were to release the controls. The instructor went on to say, "And if I say "Let the f**k go", let go immediately!". The lady interpreter said, "Ah, I have heard that many times."

The S61 operation got under way. Flying in Chinese airspace was different from any other airspace I have flown in. Like the North Sea, they flew from a base in a rig support role. I had to liaise between the Hong Kong and Chinese Civil Aviation Authorities to agree how our operation would work safely. The routes our helicopters would fly were straight into Hong Kong restricted airspace, in which jumbo jets flew extensively. The HK authorities gave us a procedure whereby we would request clearance to fly to the rig, and our pilots were to follow these instructions. The Chinese said no, they would fly where and when they wanted to, and at what height, and the jumbos could keep out of the way. We ended up with the compromise of our resident flying instructor quietly calling HK ATC to tell them of our intended flight path, and jumbos would be routed away from any possible confliction.

Our helicopters were adequate for the task in hand, but during the heat of the summer, they were restricted in how much they could carry. We discovered that it was possible to tweak the engines to give a little more power, and Sikorsky suggested a different take off technique to get the aircraft to safety speed more quickly than the standard technique. This involved coming to a high hover, very rapidly lowering the nose considerably more than normal, pulling max power to accelerate as quickly as possible and rapidly assuming the climbing attitude when the speed was achieved.

The new handling technique was developed in UK, and I spent quite a bit of time perfecting the new handling technique at Inverness Airport because Aberdeen Airport was too busy.

My next trip to Zhu Hai was with the CAA Test Pilot, the CAA Flight Test Engineer, and one of BAHL's performance engineers. Our job was to prove the handling changes were acceptable and that the engines would now provide the necessary power. We could not prove the system at our Zhu Hai base, as its runway was too short, and got permission to use a part of the taxiway at Guangzhou International Airport. The test team was BAH managing pilot, CAA test pilot, me on the jump seat, the CAA test engineer peeking over my shoulder and the BAH engineer. We let the BAH engineer get out of the helicopter to take some video of our endeavours. He was fine with this idea but got more and more nervous as several armed soldiers began to take an interest in his filming activities. This was at an airport in Communist China, after all. We managed to finish the evaluation and collect him before he was lifted by the authorities. The technique was approved, and all we had to do next was to wait for the air temperature to go above 25 degrees Celsius. The temperature stubbornly stayed below that required, and the CAA guys eventually, after several days, gave up and went home. They deputed me to do the tests, and when the temperature at last came up to that required, we went out and did the performance tests. The test flight was interesting, to say the least. In UK, when you do a test flight, it is normal to brief the local air traffic unit what you will do, and they generally let you get on with it. In China, the ATC has the final say in how you fly the trip. Before take-off, I explained what we were about to do, which involved several timed climbs to test the efficiency of the engines. The controller told me (he had some English, unlike everyone else we worked with) that I should request his permission every time I wanted to turn, climb or descend. I said that I would try to do this. However, in a test situation, you can become distracted from such requirements, and occasionally I would get a call asking me if I had turned or changed altitude. He was watching through binoculars. We eventually compromised and got the work done. So, the new-improved performance was accepted by the CAA.

Crash Position Indicators

Another safety device introduced was the Crash Position Indicator (CPI). If the aircraft crashed on land or in the sea, the shock of the impact would release the CPI, and it would begin transmitting a signal to the search authorities, via a satellite. The pilot also could release the CPI himself, e.g. if he saw survivors on the surface. We had to ensure that the device would release safely at any speed and would not hit the aircraft in its trajectory. The CPI was positioned at the rear of the tail and was released by the firing of a pyrotechnic or squib. For our trials, over a gunnery range on Salisbury Plain, we were to "fire" the CPI several times and as we could not easily replace the squib after each shot, our design engineer lay in the tail section of the fuselage, and when told to do so, would prod the release spring with a pencil. We filmed each release (no videos available then). This was an important safety improvement.

Development of Single Engine Landings Offshore

Offshore helicopters were required to carry sufficient fuel to ensure that if there is a problem on the deck they are heading for, or if an engine failed, they could fly to a suitable alternative landing site. For the S61, this meant that their alternate was a land-based landing site. The newer helicopters, like the AS332 Super Puma, were powerful enough to be able to land on a rig helipad with only one engine running, but the S61 was not. The CAA decided that helicopters with good single engine performance could use an offshore helipad to meet this requirement, which put the S61 at a disadvantage. So, BAHL's design engineers and I began to liaise with our Sikorsky opposite numbers to develop a landing technique which did not rely only on single engine power. Sikorsky came up with a technique in which the pilot would make a single engine approach so that his momentum would see the helicopter flop down on the pad. We marked out a simulated deck on a runway on Beccles airfield, and the Sikorsky test pilot and I flew many approaches as described. We got the CAA TPs along and eventually we felt that we were safe enough to venture offshore We worked hard at this technique, and we were eventually able to make the profile work.

Although the technique could be learned by a competent helicopter pilot, the CAA test pilots and I were not convinced that a pilot who was not in immediate practice could be expected to fly the technique for real. The procedure was abandoned. A few weeks later, a Federal Aviation Administration (USA version of our CAA) test pilot visited Aberdeen, and persuaded our management to let him try the technique (I was away from base at the time). He flew with one of our management pilots and nearly destroyed the aircraft by "landing" on the helipad with the tailwheel not over the landing pad. That really put the kibosh on the project. He sent me a box of Havana cigars. I think that was to apologise for nearly breaking our aircraft. However, it supported our contention that recency in the technique was essential. The cigars were appreciated by our crews and engineers. It makes the point however, that even a program which proves that something should not be done is a positive.

Development of Data link and Cockpit Voice Recorder (CVR)

Engineering techniques were constantly evolving. Our engineering department had Design Authority (hence the need for a Chief Test

Pilot) and they developed a data link system via high frequency radio transmissions which would indicate to a ground station where the aircraft was at any time the HF was switched on. On one occasion, our Flight Manager collected the test aircraft from Gatwick and returned it to Aberdeen. He forgot to switch the system off on his return, and our test engineer at Gatwick telephoned him to say to turn it off! It was a good piece of kit.

We also wanted to introduce a cockpit voice recorder and a system to record many engine and gearbox parameters. The latter required only a blank tape to be inserted into the device, and all the parameters could be studied by our engineers after landing. This gave them the ability to forecast failures in critical components. One of the recording systems worked off vibrations. A colleague of mine from RAF Odiham then ran a company which produced the vibration kit. Once, after he had been to Gatwick to pitch his system, he returned by the Airlink helicopter to Heathrow, and held his vibration system on to a part of the internal fuselage. His recording showed that one of the electric generators would fail within a few hours, and he told our engineers so. They pooh-poohed his info, and, sure enough, one of the generators did fail as forecast.

The pilots' union, BALPA, did not like the idea of a Cockpit Voice Recorder (CVR), because they were concerned that management would spy on pilots to learn what they said about individual managers. As part of the wooing process, I took a couple of the pilot union reps to the Air Accident Investigation Board (AAIB) at Farnborough for a briefing on the safety advantages of the CVR. The AAIB helped to convince the pilots of the advantages, and it was up to us managers to set up a system which would satisfy their fears. Basically, management would only listen to the tapes after an accident or incident, in the presence of the pilot concerned and a union rep. The tapes only recorded the last 30 minutes of conversation, and that was the critical time in an accident. Whilst at Farnborough, we were able to listen to the CVR recording of an incident to a BA VC10 out of Kennedy Airport in New York. We heard the crew chatting away about what they'd got up to the previous night (This was in the days before the "sterile cockpit" which forbade any conversation between the pilots which was unrelated to the aircraft operation below 10,000ft). We could hear all the radio transmissions. The recording was stereophonic, and we knew who was flying because of the questions and responses from the checklist being read out. We heard the aircraft being cleared to take off, and heard the engines, at the rear of the aircraft, spooling up for the take off run. We heard the normal chat during the acceleration, and just after lift off, a fire alarm sounded. There was complete calm on the flight deck, and the pilots went into the emergency handling techniques. Then there was a second alarm, and both engines on one side of the aircraft were on fire. We heard the captain taking over control and the necessary radio chatter. The aircraft was too heavy for a landing, and so fuel had to be dumped, but the aircraft had to be put down asap. The aircraft flew a wide circuit to land back at Kennedy, and during quiet periods, we could hear the captain's heavy breathing! The aircraft was positioned on finals, still dumping fuel, and a long approach was made. During this period, the open microphone picked up the sound of the cockpit door being opened, and the rather effeminate voice of the purser was heard to ask if there was anything he could do to help. In unison, the pilots cried, "Yes, f**k off!!". I think it was that recording which sold the CVR to the union.

Chief Pilot Technical Services

Several new helicopter types were scheduled to be brought into service, and it was clear that one FTO was not capable of the detailed acceptance of several aircraft types on to the Company Air Operators' Certificate. The FTO was elevated to Chief Pilot Technical Services, and a Technical Pilot was appointed as each new type was acquired.

The Chinook. Bringing the Boeing Vertol BV234 into Service

Our boss, Captain Jock Cameron, developed the company, and intended to expand into different types of helicopter. Shell, which had heavy passenger movement requirements between Aberdeen and the East Shetland Basin (ESB), moved its passengers by Viscount to Shetland and by S61 to the production platforms some 100 nautical miles offshore. This was a time-consuming exercise, and occasionally resulted in weather delays at Shetland. This could be damaging to morale, particularly to the shore-bound passengers. If a helicopter could be found that would enable the trip to be flown direct from Aberdeen to the East Shetland Basin, the whole operation would be much improved. In co-operation with the oil company, British Airways Helicopters approached Boeing Vertol to see if modifications could be made to the Chinook to civilianise it and give it the range required. Thus, was born the BV234. Although senior management in BAHL tried very hard to ensure the helicopter was known by this name, inevitably it was referred to as the Chinook.

However, it was markedly different from its military counterpart. It had enlarged externally mounted fuel tanks capable of permitting the aircraft to fly to the East Shetland Basin directly from Aberdeen without staging for fuel through the Shetland Islands and return to Aberdeen in the event it could not land at the offshore destination. It had a large cargo capability with ample room at the aft for baggage and cargo; it had a "floating floor" separated from the fuselage structure and with a harmonisation system whose purpose was to eliminate the effect on the passenger of the inherent vibration of the airframe, and it had a modern designer cockpit with fully coupled autopilot.

The BV234 Technical Pilot undertook the development flying programme to obtain CAA approval. Before he was appointed, I visited the Spanish Army Aviation Base at Madrid in March 78 to fly their version of the Chinook. The BV test pilot and I occupied the pilots' seats and the Spanish Army CO of the squadron was in the middle jump seat. The purpose of my trip was to establish if the

Chinook was capable of being flown down an instrument approach with various services switched off. It was proven to be the case. I flew the Chinook again when Boeing Vertol brought the military version to RAF Odiham to show the RAF. Also, when BAHL took delivery of its first BV234, it could not be flown for some time, and I had to go to Gatwick to run the engines on two occasions about a month apart, so that they did not deteriorate. One of the BV test pilots joined me on these runs.

Subsequently, I was sent to the US Army base at Fort Rucker in Georgia to brief the BV people on what was what in the North Sea environment. I also "flew" their rudimentary simulators. One had a visual presentation with a pause during climb out whilst the system changed from looking out at fields at close range to looking out over a greater range but was OK for instrument flying practice. The other was a mechanical device with a map of the sea(!) placed vertically on a wall, with a model of an oil rig glued in place. It had a helideck, but none of the BV folks were comfortable trying to land the mechanically operated CV camera which simulated the Chinook onto the deck. I made several hashes at landings, but eventually made it, to applause from the assembled management. I'm not sure I ever found out why they had this simulator.

The BV234 was successfully introduced to service in June 1981 and began the long-haul service between Aberdeen and the East Shetland Basin. Eventually BAH would operate six of these aircraft. It was a complicated aircraft, and initially had problems in meeting its regularity targets.

There were several incidents, the most spectacular non-fatal one involving an un-commanded short period vertical bounce shortly after take-off from one of the offshore platforms. It became so bad that the pilot decided to return to the platform. However, the condition deteriorated, and the decision was made to make a controlled landing on the sea. This was satisfactorily accomplished, and once on the sea, the bounce appeared to have been eliminated. As everyone on board was safe, the Captain began to water taxi towards the nearest platform, perhaps 4 miles distant. The Rescue Services were alerted, and soon helicopters and the in-field Standby Vessel were in attendance. The pilot wanted to try to save the aircraft by getting close to a platform and flying on to it. However, this was a hazardous manoeuvre, and so he ordered the passengers to abandon the aircraft, to be picked up by the rescue helicopters. It would be normal practice for the survivors to be picked up from life-rafts. Therefore, both life-rafts were launched. Unfortunately, because of the geometry of the Chinook's rotor system, even with the cyclic control centralised, the aircraft tended to move forward. So, after the life-rafts were launched and inflated, and a few passengers embarked, the drag on them caused by the forward movement of the aircraft broke their mooring lines.

The remaining passengers then were arranged so that they would exit from one of the aft emergency exits. They sat with their upper bodies outside the aircraft and their legs inside, inflated their life saving jackets and rolled backwards into the sea. The cabin attendant who controlled the whole evacuation was female, and she had a little trouble with the last passenger, who tried to insist on "Ladies First". She managed to be the last out of the passenger cabin!

In the meantime, the control irregularity returned, and the crew decided that they would not be able to fly the aircraft on to a helideck. The engines and rotors were shut down, and shortly after that the aircraft rolled over and sank. The crew were picked up safely.

The end of the Chinook came about because of a massive accident which killed all but two of the occupants, the Captain and one passenger. I think 43 soles perished. I had only recently retired from BAHL. The combining gear-box failed and caused the main rotors to de-synchronise. Although the fault was found and cured, the oil industry had lost confidence in the aircraft and it was not used again for oil support flights. BAHL sold its remaining BV234s to a Canadian logging company.

The Westland W30

Jock Cameron, BAHL MD, was a director of Westlands the helicopter manufacturer. They were developing a variant of their Naval helicopters to offer civilian passenger capacity. It was called the Westland Type 30. The helicopter company had started life making garage doors and was originally called "Westland Garages". It still retained its roots, and so the new helicopter was called the WG30. It was destined for BAHL but began to be referred to as "WD40", the penetrating oil. This wouldn't do for Jock, and he had the name changed to the "Westland 30". As FTO, I was involved with the Engineering Department in selecting the interior fit for the cockpit, and I had occasionally to visit Westland's factory to have technical meetings. On one of these trips, in Jun 80, I had to fly with their Chief Test Pilot to evaluate the aircraft in preparation for it joining our Company. This trip was in advance of the aircraft mock-up being displayed at Farnborough in 1980. I found a fairly marked vibration, particularly at low airspeeds, and commented as much in my report. A few weeks later, Jock Cameron came past my office door in Aberdeen, stopped and pointed at me, saying, "I have a bone to pick with you about your comments on vibration. I flew the aircraft only the other day, and there was no vibration evident." He was the Boss, so there was no vibration, although reference to it remained in my report. However, when I met up with the Westlands engineers at Farnborough later in the year and asked them how they had eradicated the vibration, they explained that the vibration absorber in the rotor head was able to be tuned. They literally moved the vibration which I had felt in the pilot's seat, to another part of the helicopter. So, the vibration had not been eradicated, merely hidden! I think we eventually took at least one W30 and used it on the short-range offshore trips out of Teesside, or a similarly placed airfield. It was not a great success, and the vibration constantly gave problems. Indeed, when the CAA Flight Ops Inspector flew in it to authorise it for passenger flights, he told me that the Westlands vibration was evident in the passenger cabin. He was an experienced Naval helicopter pilot, and he said that the Westlands vibration was always felt by him at the end of his nose!

On one occasion, as the W30 was making an approach to land at its base, the vibration stopped very suddenly. After landing, a major crack was found in the fuselage. That particular problem was eventually fixed.

The Westland Wessex

My role as CPTS gave me several interesting programmes to look into. The following two were in military Wessex's. One had a radar scanner fitted into the leading edge of one of its main rotor blades. This gave an interesting radar picture in the cockpit, with the scanner going at rotor speed. The other was a head down display of the flight instruments. Modern aircraft often have head up displays (HUDs), but the HDD was trialled with a view to helping the pilot to fly an instrument approach to the back of a frigate, or some such vessel. I enjoyed my exposure to both of these projects, but it would have been prohibitively expensive for BAHL to buy into the technology, even if it might have given us a slight commercial advantage over our competitors. Cost effectiveness is always important in commercial aviation.

The Sikorsky S76

BAHL bought two Sikorsky S76s. They would carry about eight passengers, and in order to make them competitive, we wanted to fly them with one pilot only. This was not good with the pilots' union, BALPA, as they felt that a single pilot's capacity would be tested. They feared that a single pilot might become overloaded in stressful situations. My concern was to help the engineers modify the aircraft to make all the electronic avionic equipment help the pilot have ample capacity to fly without a pilot's helper. It had been decided that our aircraft should be modified with fully coupled autopilot, so that it could be offered to the oil industry as a single pilot IFR (Instrument Flight Rules) machine which entailed safe flight in conditions of cloud and low visibility. After it was accepted in the USA by the Technical Pilot and the Engineering Team, it was flown to Fort Worth, in Texas, for installation of the necessary equipment. The S76 acquired by BAH was the first on the British register.

I was appointed Operations Director in 1984. I left BAHL in 1986. I thoroughly enjoyed the time I spent with the Company.

Chapter Five

Training Helicopter Pilots

Captain Tony Buckley

In any commercial flying organization, the ability of the pilot workforce to ensure safe and efficient aircraft operation is of paramount importance. In order to achieve and maintain the necessary standards of flying proficiency, commercial operators are required to provide their pilots with sufficient training for them to attain and maintain an operational standard acceptable to both the company and the relevant regulatory authority. To comply with these requirements, the North Sea Helicopter Operating Companies established dedicated Training Departments with their own Qualified Instructors and proficient Examiners.

Pilot Supply

When the North Sea helicopter operations burgeoned in the mid to late 1970s, the main supply of helicopter pilots was from the military. To gain the required number of instructed flying hours for a helicopter commercial helicopter license was, for most people, prohibitively expensive, so a more cost-effective way to learn to fly helicopters, and gain the requisite number of flying hours, was for Her Majesty the Queen to pay. As well as providing the basic skills for flying helicopters, the armed forces provided a pilot with varied and extensive experience in different operational fields and gave aviation related qualifications to a number of pilots. One of the most useful of these accomplishments was that of Qualified Helicopter Instructor (QHI).

Ex-military pilots arrived with the North Sea helicopter companies having passed the written exams and a flying test and holding a pristine new license in their eager palms. The written exams were quite extensive, but the study and instruction could be funded by the Services under their re-settlement schemes. The flying tests could be carried out by QHI's who had been given delegated examiner status by the Civil Aviation Authority (CAA). This new license then had to be validated for the type of helicopter to which the pilot had been allocated. A license validation was required for each new type a pilot wished to operate. This validation needed a flying skills test and written test based on the knowledge of the technical aspects of the new type and its systems limitations. The conduct of these tests was delegated by the CAA to approved companies training departments. The military trained instructors' qualifications were accepted by the authorities and following a check flight with a CAA Flight Examiner, these QHIs could conduct the flying tests for the initial Type Rating validation and also subsequent regular flight checks about which more later.

Conversion Courses

The newly arrived (ex-military) pilot was welcomed into the greatly more relaxed atmosphere of the civil helicopter operating company and introduced to the ground school part of the training department. In the early days of the North North Sea operations the two main helicopter types were both Sikorsky aircraft, the S58T and the ubiquitous S61N. They were both powered by two gas turbine engines and were technically more sophisticated than most of the helicopters being operated in the military at that time (not many pilots who left the services at this time had flown the Sea King). As well as learning about more complex technical systems, the concept of operating a twin-engine helicopter to civil performance requirements had to be taken on-board.

Because the S61 was the most common helicopter operated by the main North Sea companies, and because of my personal experience, the descriptions of courses, instruction and subsequent checking will be based around that aircraft. It was the most common course programme experienced by trainee North Sea pilots.

The technical systems which had to be mastered included: the two gas turbines and their fuel control systems; the main gearbox into which the turbines' power was fed with its normal and emergency lubrication capabilities; the twin hydraulic flight control systems which were used to overcome the huge forces feeding back from the main rotors when at full speed. The DC and AC electric systems with batteries, inverters and transformers; used to power lighting; flight instruments; radios; radar; and flight stability enhancing system to ease the pilot workload. The understanding of all these complexities was then confirmed by a series of test papers.

After having demonstrated a complete understanding of the workings of the helicopter, our somewhat dazed pilot moved onto the flying part of the conversion course. The S61 is certified to be flown by two crew members, a captain (P1) and a co-pilot (P2) and for a lot of pilots from the armed services, particularly the army, this concept was most unusual. The initial flying training was carried out as P2 in the left-hand Seat (LHS) with the training captain in the right. This seating configuration with the aircraft commander on the right is the opposite way round to that used in aeroplanes. (It is thought that the reason for this set up originated from the first mass produced helicopter, the Sikorsky R-4, where, in order to save weight, only a single collective lever in the centre of the cockpit was used. As the cyclic control was both heavy to operate and very sensitive, student pilots and single pilots, the majority of which were right-handed, sat in the right-hand seat.)

At the start of the flying phase of training, upon arriving at the S61, the pilot's first impression was its sheer size. The overall length from front rotor tip to tail rotor was seventy-two feet and the rotor diameter sixty-two feet. It had a reasonably spacious and comfortable cockpit with a dazzling array of flight instruments, avionics, switches, and circuit breakers, arraigned around the flight controls.

Following a detailed pre-start check list, the student then has to start the first engine. The older aircraft had a starter control which required great dexterity. A sliding sleeve around the starter handle (which was also the throttle) had to pulled down whilst at the same time a rather stiff button on the base of the handle was pushed in with the ball of the thumb, to activate the starter motor. This uncomfortable position was held until the turbine rotations reached a specified figure, at which point the whole starter handle was moved forward to inject fuel into the combustion chamber. However, the lever could not be pushed too far, or the excess fuel caused the engine to overheat, but if not far enough forward the engine would not start. There was cam on the quadrant along which the throttle moved which gave the optimum position for the start, but to engage this cam the sliding sleeve had to released upwards while the thumb continued to press the starter button. Phew!

Difficult and uncomfortable for the student and his/her thumb and nerve-racking for the instructor who had no physical control over the starting controls. With the engine now running, the rotors were started by easing the throttle forward to accelerate the engine, releasing the rotor brake and continuing the forward movement of the throttle until the optimum Rotor RPM was reached. Next, the second engine was started requiring the same manual dexterity. All the other aircraft systems now have to be switched on and checked after which the aircraft is ready for flight.

Despite its size, the S61 is a stable and responsive helicopter to fly. The student is very soon able to advance onto learning how to cope with the various system failures which can occur in flight. Having two engines, the S61 can maintain level flight following the failure of a single power unit, albeit with a slight reduction in speed depending upon the weight of the aircraft. However, at most operational weights, when the helicopter slows down and loses transitional lift (the lift benefit of the airflow through the rotor disc), a single engine will not have enough power to maintain height, so landings have to be made with some forward speed.

Also, during the take-off, until the helicopter reaches a certain height/speed combination, continued flight cannot be guaranteed so there is a need to re-land with some forward speed. Engine failures are simulated by the training captain retarding one of the two throttles to a minimum setting without actually shutting down the engine. As well being able to handle the failure of an engine in all phases of flight there are many other system failures to be covered, all of which mean the training captain having to reduce the standards of safety provided by duplex systems. The above exercises are also carried out at night and for the S61 its amphibious capability is demonstrated by the student carrying out landing on water. For any pilot putting a large flying machine down on the surface of a lake or the sea is totally alien but quite exhilarating.

Included in the handling exercises required for a budding North Sea pilot is the training to enable him to land on the helidecks of the rigs and/or platforms based offshore. Ideally these landings and take-offs should be experienced both in daylight and at night, however, in the northern part of the UK in winter it can be dark for most of the day and then in summer practically daylight for twenty-four hours. The techniques demonstrated and then practiced offshore had been developed to minimize the effect of an engine failure on the latter stages of the approach to the deck and also during taking-off. The S61 still needs maximum power from two engines both during these stages of the approach and during the first part of the take-off, and the techniques used tried to minimize the exposure to the effects of any loss of power in these phases of flight.

After about ten hours of dual instruction the student is tested as to ability fly the helicopter type and cope with the failures above. With a successful result from both the flight test and the written exam the details are submitted to the CAA and the type rating is added to the pilot's license.

Line Training

Our ex-military pilot would arrive at his allocated new base, most likely Aberdeen or Shetland, clutching a bright shiny license with the necessary type rating included. He is now ready to start operational flying or 'line flying'. An Initial Line Check is carried out where all aspects of the preparation for and the conduct of a flight with passengers on board are checked out. This would include: flight planning; calculation of the aircraft weight and balance; the fuel required; an examination of the Aircraft Technical Log; pre-flight check of the helicopter exterior and interior with particular emphasis on the emergency exits and survival equipment carried. Normal start-up checks are carried out, and after the rotors are running with the electrical power being generated, the radios, flight instruments and the navigation aids are checked.

The main navigational equipment carried in the early days of North Sea operations comprised a Non-Directional Beacon (NDB) the VHF Omnidirectional Range (VOR) and the Decca Navigator. The first two consisted basically of needles which pointed in the direction of a ground-based radio beacon, the NDB with a longer range but less accuracy and the VOR limited to 'line of sight' range, which for usual helicopter operating heights was up to 100 nautical miles.

The Decca Navigator

The Decca Navigator System was based on a series of 'chains' around the world consisting of a master and two or three slave stations. The transmissions from these stations could be analyzed by the on-board receiver to determine where the receiver was along each of the hyperbolic lines from the transmitting stations, thereby determining an accurate position. This information could be further processed and shown on a moving map display located above the instrument panel in the cockpit.

Initializing the Decca system required the selection of the correct key for the chain being used in the area of operation, and then zeroing each 'Deccometer' by positioning a 'cheese' (a triangular wire shaped like a segment of cheese) over a rotating pointer when the pointer paused over a reading. This was done for each of the red, green and purple slaves. When correctly set up the system was very accurate, and it was the only form of accurate navigation available to North Sea helicopters when beyond the range of the VORs. The Decca system could also be used for precision approaches to airfields where no other aids were available.

Initial Line Check

With the system and pre-take-off checks completed a non-revenue flight (Initial Line Check) was carried out possibly to an offshore installation to assess the candidate's suitability to be part of the crew for passenger carrying flight.

For the experienced Line Training Captain (LTC), the first few flights with a newly fledged P2 were worse than being in the cockpit on his own! Not only does the LTC have to do all the pre-flight work whilst at the same time explaining all the nuances of each aspect, but he then has to watch every single move by the new co-pilot to ensure that every button, switch or lever is pushed, pulled or pressed in the correct way. And then there is the landing on an offshore rig or platform. Certain wind directions and obstructions around the helideck could dictate that the landing has to be flown by the pilot in the left-hand seat which means that that the captain in the right-hand seat will have difficulty in seeing where the limits of the deck and its critical markings are. The non-handling pilot (in this case the captain) uses the throttles to maintain the correct Rotor RPM using his left hand which is therefore away from the collective lever until the latter stages of the approach. Hard work for the LTC especially at night in storm force winds with rain or snow.

Instrument Flying

In the early days of North Sea helicopter operations (1970 to approximately 1978) there was no Helicopter Instrument Rating. This did not prevent the ex-military pilot with a service instrument flying qualification flying in cloud and poor visibility provided that the weather conditions offshore and back at base did not preclude a visual approach and landing. To allow for procedural flying on instruments and to comply with the Instrument Flight Rules (IFR) the CAA could award a 'Certificate of Competency on Instruments' which was awarded when the pilot completed a flying test the contents of which were identical to those required for the award of the Aeroplane Instrument Rating. The flight test comprised a departure from an airfield; an Airways section flown between two or more aeronautical beacons; a 'racetrack' shaped holding pattern at a specific height over a beacon taking exactly four minutes; a 'non-precision' approach again based on a beacon; a 'precision' approach known as an ILS (Instrument Landing System); and a missed approach procedure from one of the approaches during which the candidate had to manage a simulated single engine failure. All this test was flown by the pilot solely on instruments, with the windows on his side being blanked out by screens and operating as a single pilot with no assistance from the 'safety pilot' in the other seat.

The Holding Pattern

As well as demonstrating the flying skill during the test (height keeping ±100ft and speed ±10knots throughout the flight) the holding pattern required some mental gymnastics to enable the helicopter to arrive back at the nominated beacon flying up the correct track and arriving overhead exactly four minutes from the start, all of which has to be done using only a needle on the compass which points directly towards the beacon being used. In still air, the aircraft passes directly over head the beacon, turns out-bound through 180° at 30° of bank, taking one minute, then flies outbound on a track parallel to the specified inbound track for a further minute, another 180° turn back towards the beacon on exactly the correct track and arriving back overhead again after four minutes. BUT there is no such thing as still air when flying at heights of 2,000 to 5,000 feet. Therefore, an assessment of the wind must be made when approaching the beacon and an adjustment made to the track flown on the outbound leg for any crosswind, and the length of time outbound adjusted for any tailwind/headwind before turning back to the beacon. There were various ways of doing this, and pilots had their different preferred methods, but it all had to be done with someone leaning over your shoulder critically watching your every move. No wonder the helicopter Instrument Rating was considered the most difficult flying qualification of all to achieve.

Recurrent Checks

A commercial pilot's life is bedeviled by a seemingly continuous round of checks and tests. Every six months a check is carried out to ensure a pilot's competency to handle the helicopter safely under normal conditions and also to be able to manage a series of simulated system malfunctions. This is done by the pilot flying visually during daytime initially, and then on every alternate check whilst flying at night. The aircraft is loaded with ballast (for instance, sandbags or rubber blocks) up to a weight equivalent of 90 per cent of the maximum take-off weight for the prevailing atmospheric conditions; this is to provide a more realistic representation of the normal operating weight on a commercial flight. A training captain occupies the other crew seat and at any stage during the flight is liable to simulate the failure of one of the engines or of any of the duplicated systems on the helicopter. There is an element of risk involved in conducting check flights in this way as the redundancy of the systems being failed has been removed. Because these check flights are usually carried out at the Company's operating base they are known as 'Base Checks'. Also, at six-monthly intervals, the pilot's instrument flying proficiency is checked. Having been isolated from the outside world by screens on his side of the cockpit, he is tasked with flying a non-precision approach and an ILS solely by reference to the flight instruments and at the same time dealing with engine failures and other assorted system failures. On each alternative six-monthly instrument- check the Instrument Rating is revalidated by the inclusion of an airways section and the carrying out of a standard four- minute Holding Pattern. Assuming the pilot under test successfully achieved a pass standard in all sections of the test. A failure in any section would result in a referral for further training.

Line Checks

Every twelve months the pilot is assessed on a commercial flight to ensure that it is conducted in accordance with the Standard Operating Procedures as laid down in the Company's Operations Manual. There are no simulated emergencies on these flights. These flights are known as 'Line Checks'.

Aircraft Availability

All training flights i.e. initial type rating instruction; instrument training; recurrent base and instrument flying checks, required a helicopter to be taken away from the commercial flying programme. These training flights therefore not only cost the company the regular running costs of flying a helicopter (fuel, maintenance, wear and tear, etc.) but also the lost revenue which could have been generated on a commercial flight. The difficulty of obtaining an aircraft for training during the busy weekday periods led to training being carried out at weekends and sometimes in the evenings. Even so, a training flight would occasionally be cancelled to allow a revenue producing flight to take place. One answer to this, during a spell of intensive instrument training when all pilots were being Instrument Rated, was to take a helicopter and a selection of candidates and de-camp to another airfield from where it would be difficult and time wasting to re-position the helicopter back to base. The airfields needed to have instrument facilities required for training, and favourites were Inverness and Teesside. Of course, another solution would be the provision of a simulator.

Chapter Six

The Joy of Simulators

Captain Peter Harris

It is difficult to remember those days in which some form of simulation was not available for just about every action we are involved in nowadays. We have had aircraft and flight simulators around for some time now and they are taken for granted but in the sphere of the helicopter they are a fairly recent arrival. Those who underwent instrument flight training in the sixties and before will recall the Link Trainer, some with affection but most I would surmise (at least for those without a nostalgic romantic streak in them) with a feeling of indifference.

The Link Trainer was probably as far as most helicopter pilots got before the end of the seventies by way of exposure to flight simulators. Simulator programmes for personal computers were dreams away.

In the airline world though it was different. Aeroplanes had long been associated with dedicated simulators and although nowadays they would seem primitive in comparison with today's versions, they offered great advantages in safety and depth of training.

The 1970s saw a great expansion in the North Sea offshore oil industry and to support it a much- enlarged fleet of machines (The Sikorsky S61N was the standard preferred workhorse) was required plus the necessary flight crews to man them. These crews all required some degree of training although as almost all were ex-military pilots most of them required a minimum of training to be able to fly as VFR qualified pilots, whereas the training requirements for those from different backgrounds varied according to their experience. Nevertheless, all training had to be done on the aircraft which meant that aircraft had to be taken away from commercial availability from time to time to enable the training to be done. Inevitably accidents, mostly not serious ones, did occur and then repairs had to be effected before the helicopter was put back on line. I recall incidences of inadvertent wheels up landings.

Training was completed at a minimum of 90 per cent MTOW (Maximum Take-Off Weight) to give a realistic single engine performance which usually required the aircraft had to be ballasted up. On one occasion I recall a ballast of 1,000 lb being required, which in effect meant loading 20 X 50lb sandbags on board. The resulting single engine performance was less than encouraging, which of course was not discovered until the required single engine landing was carried out. When the ballast was checked it transpired that 20 X 50 *kg* bags had been loaded and although no damage resulted in this case it was evident that something more serious might have happened. There was always that moment when the training captain pulled back the appropriate engine speed lever and hoped/ wondered if the remaining engine would deliver as advertised. The real white-knuckle test was taking off from a platform at night and then deliberately failing an engine. One hoped that in addition to possibility of the engine not performing, the pilot under training had really listened to the pre- flight brief.

It wasn't all grind though and the way in which the training weekends were set up could at times result in a battle of wits with the senior management. They obviously wanted us to do our training as efficiently and cheaply as possible, whereas we determined to enjoy ourselves if possible. It led to occasions when, sequestered at such exotic and idyllic places as Inverness where we had been told that the bills for our meals would be met without question BUT that did not include any drinks, that mysterious 'Carafes of extra vegetable' appeared on the bills. On one occasion a member of the accounts staff had been sent with us to ensure that the evening meals were ordered from the *'table d'hote'* menu and not the *'a la carte'*. However, we had noticed that the table *d'hote* menu finished early and so we delayed entry to the dining room until just after that set time. The hotel staff were on our side for that and very shortly after the 'enemy' surrendered and departed, leaving us in peace. Time spent as a short-haul pilot in the RAF was obviously not wasted.

The real push on training came in the mid 1970s when it was seen that an IFR capable operation was going to be essential. Some pilots had had some instrument training and had possibly held military instrument ratings. Others were not so fortunate and needed to be trained from scratch on, in most cases, the S61 helicopter, an extremely costly and time-consuming task. The pilots to be trained could be detailed; the aircraft could be allocated (subject to commercial requirements) but the weather could be fickle and as result days were often lost and the training schedules suffered accordingly. In the early part of that decade the decision was taken by British Airways Helicopters (BAH) to buy and operate a flight simulator, not just a device for procedural training and, maybe IFR training, but a VFR and IFR capable machine which would accurately replicate the performance of the S61N helicopter. The contract was awarded to Rediffusion, based in Crawley and close to BAH head office (the Beehive at Gatwick on what became the site for the CAA). The movement platform was based on those currently available and operating on the aeroplane simulators currently in use by airlines and that gave a full six axis replication of movement. An aircraft cockpit and control cabin were designed and built allowing for on-board instruction and then of course there was the software. Computers of that time were still large affairs and, thankfully, beyond my description but a suitable operating programme had to be written.

Helicopters of that vintage were largely designed using the TLAR principle – *That Looks About Right*. The basic performance of the aircraft was well-documented and proved there were many grey areas surrounding the actual response rates to control inputs and the effects of those inputs when put against the actual movement of the machine. For example, if the cyclic was moved forward through X degrees at a rate of Y degrees/second then what would the aircraft actually do. We could experience it in the aircraft itself by observing it, but when this had to be transferred to translatable data (remembering that there was no inertia to deal with) then the results could be very different, and this difference needed quantifying. It was decided that the best way to resolve this was to send a pilot each week to Rediffusion to attempt to get a satisfactory result. A group of pilots were accordingly briefed and each Monday morning the 'Duty Pilot, would travel to Gatwick, returning on Friday evening well satisfied with a good week's work. The next Monday the next pilot would travel down, sample the previous weeks work, usually disagree with what had been achieved and spend the rest of the week sorting it out. This went on for several weeks but by the end of 1977 a satisfactory level of accuracy had been achieved, the CAA had flown and given approval and the simulator was shipped to Aberdeen to be installed for operation, commencing service in early 1978.

The impact on training was evident right from the beginning. Initially it was given approval for three out of four annual checks to be completed on the sim with the fourth, a Visual Base Check, to be flown in an aircraft. All VFR training could be completed in the sim with only a minimum requirement for aircraft training at initial conversion. Instrument training was also possible but with the Instrument Rating Test having to be flown in the aircraft. A huge load off the shoulders of the Operations staff in making aircraft available and of course the flexibility and reliability that the Training Staff enjoyed made the task of training so much easier now that the weather factor had been removed from the equation.

It would be wrong to suspect that it all went smoothly to start with. Some of the Training Captains did not really believe that safe and accurate training could be achieved using a simulator. The various faults that the simulator was programmed for were selected by pressing a designated button, but it was possible to press the wrong button in error, causing the simulated aircraft to move through hyper space at warp speed goodness-knows- what, ending up anywhere but the right place. However, as we became more proficient the number of errors reduced and it became very obvious that system or component failures that could not be replicated on the actual aircraft without the risk of damage or loss of life, could be shown safely. The pilots responded very positively, and the levels of proficiency and confidence were raised.

One particular event stays with me. One system failure that was unique to the S61 was a Flex Drive Failure. With this problem it was possible to mis-diagnose the fault and end up landing and over speeding the affected engine and rotor head (I think that that is correct. I haven't had to think about this for almost forty years). On one occasion I had introduced it to a pilot. The first time he reacted as expected and the engine over-speeded. The second time the problem was analysed, understood, and the correct action taken to contain it. It should be mentioned that this was not a common occurrence but on his very next flight the flex drive failed. He handled it in text-book fashion, managing the risk, and no damage was done, a saving of many thousands of pounds.

It was of course possible to programme intentionally a condition that could determine the flying characteristics. There was a Training Captain (TC) who disliked the simulator immensely. On one occasion the previous TC leaving the simulator had, unannounced, selected a 4,000lb weight hung onto the load hook by a long line. The aircraft could be hovered but as it moved forward the 'long line' extended to its length and the simulator simulated a crash to the ground. Down came the hydraulics, the door at the rear of the cabin opened and a furious TC came out swearing that he would never fly the thing again. The previous TC who had recently vacated stepped in, just in case there was anything that he could do to help, quietly removed the load, lifted off, transitioned and then re-landed. Piece of cake; can't see what the problem is. Handing back control to his colleague he quietly reset the load and vacated the cabin. You can imagine the rest. Hydraulics on, legs extended, some movement followed by a crash and the system lowering. The TC concerned came out storming and swearing he was definitely going to resign if he had to fly that thing again. However, this time the system was reset (without saying what the problem had been) and the rest of his session passed uneventfully. I don't believe he ever did learn, but if he reads this and twigs what was done to him, I whole-heartedly apologise (on behalf of the perpetrator of course).

After the advent of the S61 simulator at Aberdeen other companies followed suit and very shortly afterwards there was a BV234 (civil Chinook model) simulator in Aberdeen and an AS332L simulator in Stavanger, both of which offered huge improvements over the early S61 model. The last simulator that I had personal experience of was the S76 sim in Palm Beach, Florida but that was some time into the future. Overall, I spent several thousand hours operating, testing and teaching in simulators and I really don't see how we could have managed without them.

Since those early days, the world of simulators has changed almost beyond recognition. Gone are the black/white CGI images presented on three screens, giving a sharp but limited night view of the outside world. It is now replaced with wrap around screens with full daylight presentations. As later models have been modelled the amount of information available to the manufacturer has increased and computer speeds have increased considerably. Nevertheless, I was proud to be part of that early team and very proud of the way in which we pushed the use of the Helicopter Flight Simulator to develop safer flying techniques and the understanding of the aircraft involved.

Chapter Seven

Training Cabin Crew

Bonny's Story

My name is Bonny Westgate. I joined British Airways helicopters on the 4 August 1980. Little did I know that the next few years would be some of the happiest and saddest of my life. I had spent eight years in Detmold West Germany where I worked in air-traffic control as an Assistant. We were supposed to be the first defence if and when the Russians came over the hill. As there were a hell of a lot of hills in North Rhine, Westphalia, I always hoped the Russians would choose a hill a long way from me and so it proved to be. Nonetheless I had to go through all kinds of security checks up to and including atomic correspondence, all very James Bond.

One day an American voice came over the radio. I asked for his call sign and aircraft type but the response I received was 'I got a lot of blade and I'm coming down'. This was my first meeting with members of the 'Screaming Eagle Squadron' from Mainz, who had arrived in a CH47 'Chinook'. It was an enjoyable exercise just watching them. They are referred to as the 'tip of the spear', their motto being 'Rendezvous with Destiny'. That was my first introduction to the Chinook. It would not be my last.

I lived in Germany for eight years before deciding that I wanted to return to the UK, essentially to get onto the housing ladder. Having taken advantage of a very good savings scheme in Germany, I had enough savings for a deposit to buy a house, but where to go?

The North Sea oil boom had taken off, so I decided to head to Aberdeen, driving from Detmold to Zeebrugge before the ferry crossing, followed by the long drive north. It was not long before the police stopped me for not displaying a tax disc – they don't have them in Germany as its included in your insurance. He still told me I had to report to a police station and looked at me very oddly when he asked me what I had covered up on the back seat of the car. I told him it's my budgie, Snoopy, but he still asked to see it.

I was staying with a friend in Aberdeen for a while when I noticed an advert in the paper for an Operations Assistant at British Airways Helicopters. I applied for and got the job and was to start work on August 4th. The year was 1980.

I spent the next year working in operations, which, after Germany, was rather tame but a good challenge all the same. One day I heard a rumour that BAH were going to buy six new Chinook helicopters from Boeing-Vertol and that these very large aircraft would be designed to carry forty-four passengers. Aviation law stipulates that any aircraft carrying more than nineteen passengers requires cabin-crew, so I put in an application to join. To say that my application was received with horror, is to put it mildly. The one place that was completely male dominated at that time was the North Sea.

There are several reasons for this. The sleeping accommodation provided on the rigs were in either two- or four- man berths so, if a female was stuck offshore where would they sleep? It would mean that two or four men had to give up their berths as there was no contingency plan for an extra person to sleep somewhere.

Also, the guys working offshore had dreamed up all kinds of tough sounding names. The one they favoured the most was 'North Sea Tigers', so you get the idea. An eight stone, five-foot-four-inch girl could not possibly survive the rigorous North Sea, could she? It was a freezing cold benighted place, terrible weather all the time, hurricane winds, you name it. Absolutely no place for the gentle sex. The truth was that, when we were the first aircraft out in the morning, on a sunny day – (yes they do have them in Aberdeen) – you felt the whole of the North Sea belonged to you. It was very beautiful, and you really could see for miles and miles.

The training course was highly technical and demanding, covering everything from airframe, electrical, fuel and hydraulic systems, engines, loading, meteorology, fire and smoke training and then the Dunker. The dreaded Dunker! The Chief Pilot at the time thought I could be the token female and would not listen to all the horror stories dreamed up about what could happen to me and so I was accepted.

I started an eight-week training course. The BV234LR, as the Chinook was called, was the civilian version of the military CH47 that I had first met in Germany. LR stands for long range and it had two very powerful Avco Lycoming engines.

The cabin could seat forty-four passengers and three crew – two pilots and the Cabin Attendant. There was a proper toilet, and a small galley. All the seats reclined and above them were overhead bins for cabin bags, the same as you will find in a commercial aircraft. There was a music system playing through a library of tapes. At the back of the aircraft and housed within the ramp were two huge bins for the large bags the guys needed for their stint offshore. They did not travel lightly.

All in all, the BV234 was a very comfortable and well – equipped aircraft, the most modern on the North Sea. There were two 36-man life rafts. After the classroom technical lessons, we moved onto weather and fuel contamination, and we had to be able to spit. When an offshore fuel sample was checked by drawing it through a test syringe, it would turn blue if there was water contamination. At the end of the test you needed to spit on the test capsule to make sure it was working.

Survival was next. We were taken to a purpose-built facility, Robert Gordon's Institute of Offshore Technology. This is where the 'Dunker' lives, the scourge of many a man. If you failed the course, you could not work offshore, end of story. In my many times there I saw a lot of 6ft men in tears because they just couldn't face The Dunker. You sat in a mock-up of a helicopter cabin with an open, grill style floor. The Dunker drill consisted of a slow capsize, fast capsize and black capsize. You heard through the PA, 'Ditching! Ditching!

Ditching!' which is enough to scare the bejesus out of you I promise you. The 'cabin' was then lowered into the water which was only six degrees (i.e. perishing) and came in slowly in the first run. The person in the cabin with us said the water would stop at chest height. Most of the guys I was with were nearly six feet tall. I am five-feet-four, so you get the picture? Six degrees will take your breath away but the trouble is you are supposed to take a breath before the cabin rolls over and you feel like you're in a washing machine. Over you go until your upside down in the water and you are supposed to count '1001 1002' etc. until you get to 1007. The divers who are under water with you – and have breathing apparatus by the way – are watching you. If they think you are cheating they make you do it again, so it's not worth it. Everyone watched me like a hawk no matter what I did, so I had zero chance of getting away with anything. The funny thing was, we were asked before getting into the Dunker, who could swim and who couldn't. If you couldn't swim you wore a red hard hat, if you could swim it was blue. Obviously, the others smelt some sort of leniency if they said they couldn't swim. As I'm a confident swimmer my hat was blue and I was left alone while the red brigade had a diver right next to them. The dunker witnessed many failures, but thankfully I wasn't one of them.

Survival training came next, in the pool which had a wind and wave machine with a particularly horrible misogynist man for an instructor who took an instant dislike to me. We had to swim the entire length of an Olympic-size pool wearing cotton overalls to a life raft at the far end with the wind and wave machine going full belt. Just as I finally reached the life raft, I heard 'man overboard'

At the other end of the pool the horrible man bellowed at me, 'Oi you Little Girl, there's a bleeding man drowning here. Get back here now.' So back I went again to reach a dummy called Fred who weighed ten stone. He was also dressed as we were and I had to grab hold of him and start swimming back again. Along this now tortuous path walked the man shouting 'What's the matter Little Girl, too tough for you? Thought you could just walk in here and act like real men?' I just contented myself with grinning at him which incensed him even more, as I knew it would.

I reached the life raft and dragging Fred with me. You were supposed to help the weakest in first, me in this case. The 36-man life raft has two chambers which sit about six feet above you and it's really very difficult to get into it, especially if you have to get in first to help everybody else. That is no mean feat when you've swum the length of that pool three times!

My colleagues were also at the raft but the instructor decided I had to get in first. Leaving Fred with one of them, I tried to get in, which is easier said than done. You can't jump in with nothing to stand on so you try to grab the top chamber which is bendy and slippery and by the time you have fallen back in a few times, swallowing water every time, you really are exhausted. However, my colleagues decided I was going in that raft one way or another, so with all of them grabbing a part of me I was heaved up and thrown into the raft. Interesting experience. Eventually, everybody finally got into the raft. We then had to close off the door to keep the sea out. To do this there are male and female clips that match up, quite why they are black and not dayglo I have no idea. Once inside and secure, you stream the drogue, which is a sea anchor, and close up as tightly as you can to protect everyone from the cold.

At this point, we were feeling pleased with ourselves, Mr Unpleasant turned a fireman's hose on us! We had been in six degrees of water for about three hours by now and this assault was very unwelcome. The deluge was hammering on the outside of the life-raft to deafening effect. Fortunately, the clips held so not a lot of water came into the raft.

There is a lot of equipment in a life-raft. One such was a heliograph, an ingenious piece of kit. Just a small piece of metal with a Christian shaped cross cut out of it. If you had to use it in a survival situation, you shone it into the sun, if there was any, the centre of the cross was where you were, it could be seen for many miles. Allegedly the heliograph was made by North American Indians, the ones that scalp you! There were also various sized bungs for repairing holes, a bellows, patches and plenty of drinking water. There was also first aid kit, a survival book but no food as we expected to be rescued long before becoming hungry. For this we relied on the SARBE (Search and Rescue Beacon Equipment). As soon as everyone was in the raft you secured it inside and threw it overboard. It would right itself and begin transmitting your position. If anyone picked up a SARBE signal if was reported immediately to the coastguard, and the search and rescue coordination centre. SARBE's have saved many thousands of lives. There was a speech facility on it as well but use of this could shorten the battery life. However, if a rescue craft was nearby but in fog for example, it was very handy to be able to speak to someone.

We also had flares in the life-raft, one end knobbly for night use with an illuminated flare, the other end was smooth for day use emitting, usually, orange smoke.

We continued training with the fire service, which was great fun, and then went offshore to learn about fuel contamination. This is where spitting came in useful. Fuel would be drawn into a syringe from the tanks, if the syringe remained yellow it would indicate no water was present in the fuel, but once tested you spat on the sample which would then turn green to indicate the syringe worked as there was now water in the sample.

The first time I went offshore (June, blowing 30 knots, just a breeze really) I was amazed at the size of the rigs, which really were a superb feat of engineering. We went out in a Chinook to the Brent oil field and this was a learning curve for all of us, including the pilots. We all wore our usual BA uniform complete with high heel shoes (just for me not the boys). I hadn't taken more than three steps when the HLO (Helideck Landing Officer) told me I couldn't wear them in case I made a spark with my heel. He went away and came back with the smallest pair of safety boots he could find, which of course were still miles too big for me. I looked ridiculous clomping around in boots with my summer dress on. The decking on an oil rig is a metal grill construction so you could see straight through it. As I looked down below me, there were dozens of faces looking up! Before we left the rig that day, the whole of the North Sea had received message, 'There is a girl here and she is wearing grey silk stockings'. Apparently, rumours had been rife that a girl was coming out on the Chinook but nobody believed it. The North Sea Tigers were still talking about it years afterwards. We all thoroughly enjoyed our day offshore and when it was time to leave, I was given perfume and the smokers were given cigarettes. You can buy certain amounts of duty free offshore as the installations are outside territorial waters. However, all the rigs were definitely 'dry', alcohol being a big no- no. We really enjoyed the lunch we were given and it would have put a five star restaurant to shame. As all the guys do is work, sleep and eat, the food had to be good.

I asked the HLO for my shoes in return for the boots but he looked very sheepish, eventually admitting that they had been raffled, so back to Aberdeen I went in a pair of roustabout's boots!

Over the years I came to realise that these North Sea Tigers had very soft hearts. They used to show films offshore of an ('Ahem') let's call it of an educational nature. The guys were charged a fee for watching these films and the money was sent to various children's charities in Aberdeen. I'm quite sure the recipients of this largesse never knew how the money was raised.

There is a huge and very heavy-duty net on the helideck on the rigs covering the area which the helicopter would land on. This was used as an anti-skid device. If water, fuel or oil was spilt it could mean disaster for the aircraft. Salt water will freeze if the temperature is low enough and when the seas were really rough, the sea would come up over the helideck. In really bad weather, especially in very high winds, a rope would be tied to the net, the other end tied to the door leading up to the helideck, the men would then have something to hang onto as they got on and off the aircraft. We did this by putting one returning passenger on board, then letting one man off to keep the weight on the aircraft. When I was out on the helideck, I always made sure the zip on my survival suit was done up properly. If wind or air got into the suit it could blow you up like a balloon and over the side you would go. On a semi- submersible the helideck was about 60 feet above the sea but on a fixed production platform like BPs Magnus, it was about 400 feet plus above the sea.

One day landing back at Aberdeen onto a remote stand, I'd just said my forty-four goodbyes to my passengers when I heard someone shouting. I looked over to a S61 on stand and noticed engineers running. Engineers do not normally run so I knew something was going on. I ran across the pan and up to the suit room where our survival suits were kept. Mine was easy to spot as it was silver. I also had a black one like everybody else, while the offshore workers had orange suits. I grabbed my suit and raced back to the S61, which was immediately airborne. I still had on my dress uniform and while everyone else was busy laying down a rubberised floor which was used for winching to save salt-water sloshing about on an aluminium floor, I stripped out of my uniform and donned my immersion suit. I had no idea where we were going or what the problem was. It turned out one of our S61s had suffered an engine failure and the other one was oscillating which meant the rotor RPM was fluctuating outside limits, so an immediate landing was required. Fortunately, the aircraft was not far offshore. We made contact with our aircraft and flew alongside them so the passengers could see we were there. The aircraft landed safely and all passengers were transferred to us. The pilots stayed with the aircraft while some engineers flew out to it and later brought it safely home.

A few months later, we were interviewed by the local radio station and I was completely dumbfounded to be asked, 'I believe you don't mind getting undressed in public, I bet there were a few comments?' To which I replied, 'No, nobody took any notice, which was true because everyone was so busy. Peter Garland, our supervisor, had told the guy in the radio station what had happened that day including my stripping off. I think the whole of Aberdeen heard that broadcast judging by the number of comments I received. I was given a tape of the broadcast and I have it to this day.

A word on survival suits. We didn't wear them in the summer as they were very hot and had a habit of creeping up your back and pinching your skin but another helicopter operator complained so we had to wear them after that. When we were measured for our suits, we were given a picture of a stick man and told to measure from here to here to here etc. Now given that there is a slight difference between boys and girls, I was really stumped to be asked "What is your inside leg measurement?" I've never been asked that before, so I was not at all sure where to measure to and from! I went into the Pilots' Crew Room and asked, in about three seconds flat there were about a dozen pilots surrounding me all fighting for the tape measure! There was a lot of laughter until a voice boomed out, "What the hell's going on here?" I looked round and there stood the Chief Pilot who looked at me and said, "Oh, it's you, I might have known." Nice!

The fact that the suits made you look like a man came in handy on a few occasions. We were part of a military operation at sea called JATE and we supplied them with the every day-to-day things they needed. In those days, if you flew on Valentine's Day on a BA aircraft, you were given heart shaped chocolates and we had some in the office. We were going out to a naval ship with supplies on a Sunday so I thought I'd take them the Sunday papers. I never met anyone offshore who didn't long for the daily papers. I also took some of the chocolates. I was winched down onto this ship with a line of their personnel watching to see how the civvies did it. Very well indeed thank you very much! I kept my visor down on my helmet and once on the deck, walked over to some sailors, lifted my visor and said "I've brought you the papers". Well, they jumped back about six feet.

Another time with the same exercise, I and my colleague, Tudor, were doing a high line transfer on to a submarine. There were two men atop the conning tower, one holding a table tennis bat, one side red, the other green. Green to say come on, red to say stand-off. We had the door locked open on the S61 and I was sitting in the door to tell Tudor, who was further back in the door space, when to fire the high line according to the colour of the bat. I was also trying to give the pilot a running commentary to con him into position. As we were very close to the submarine, it was easy to lip-read what one was saying to the other which was, "Bloody 'ell, there's a bloke up there with lipstick on!" I just couldn't resist giving him a very theatrical wink. I will never forget the look on his face.

Rockall is a pinnacle of granite sticking out of the Atlantic Ocean, some 279km north west of Stornaway. Just about all of the countries in the northern hemisphere have claimed it at one time or another but, on the 18 September 1955, the Captain of HMS Vidal raised the Union Jack on Rockall and claimed it for the UK. A plaque bearing this legend was bolted to the rock but this has now gone – odd the things that people steal.

In 1971 a light beacon was put on Rockall, which is battery operated and which needs changing periodically. To do this some guys from the Scottish mountaineering team are winched down onto the rock where they slung a rope around some mountaineering bolts that were already in place, leaving supplies for the next person to complete the job – and that is where I came in. We were going to winch somebody down on to the rock, leave him to do his job, and pick him up the next day. As we would be critical on fuel after dropping him off, we would only have minutes to get him down before we had to get back to Stornaway. I briefed this man very carefully to make sure he knew we could not hang around hovering over Rockall. I told him once he was sitting in the door and we were ready to go, I would tap him on the shoulder to get his attention. As he wouldn't be able to hear me with the door open, I would give him a thumbs up to which he would respond the same and off he would go. I was the winch operator that day and all was going well until the critical moment, when this chap decided to freeze. The captain was yelling in my ear asking if he was on the way and I knew we only had moments before we just had to go, so I gave him a gentle nudge to help him out. He didn't look very happy with me when we went out to pick him up the next day.

There is little in the way of trees in the Shetland Isles – the wind flattens them. It's quite bare really. One of the farmers there gave

BA some land to build a property on, provided that we kept flying our Highlands and Islands route which we do to this day. BA built a sort of big cabin for want of another word, above a spectacular beach which looked like the Caribbean until you put your feet in the water. At Sumburgh there was a portacabin hotel with about ten bedrooms, a bar and a restaurant. It was a very popular place as there was nowhere else to go. It provided accommodation for pilots, Air Traffic Controllers, firemen, and ground handlers. At the bar there was a dart-board but the TV signal was awful, but you could get a meal there or down in the restaurant. It was a staging post really and we would be detached there for a week at a time and fly in and out of Sumburgh to the rigs, which was a much quicker helicopter journey than from Aberdeen as you were already half-way there.

My time on the North Sea was great, I have nothing but fond memories of it. I've been asked so many times was I ever scared? No is the answer to that. Cold, tired, fed up but never scared. The sad part is that I lost too many very good friends who died too soon. Bill Deacon, who, after rescuing 10 men from the 'Green Lily', lost his own life. For his heroic actions he was awarded the George Cross. Mick Walton who was killed in the Chinook accident FC on the 8 November 1986. Brian Johnson and others.

To all the people I met along the way, and to those great guys offshore who never forgot my birthday, thanks for the memories. It was great fun. I remember you all very fondly.

Chapter Eight

A Day in the Life...

Captain Peter Saxton

The next day started the night before. The BBC nine o'clock weather was always an interesting indication of the sort of day you were in for. The wind could go from calm to 60 knots and it was still normal 'ops'. The visibility could go from gin-clear to fog and it was still 'normal ops'. The cloud-base could be predicted at 500 feet – still normal ops. It could be predicted as low as 200 feet above airfield level; still normal ops. For take-off it was the ability to see two runway lights each spaced 50 meters apart so a safe transition from the hover to forward flight could be achieved before pulling up into 'the clag'.

Except that it was not as simple as that. The thing about North Sea weather was not so much that it often produced challenging flying conditions – it was that it could be rapidly and unpredictably changeable.

The alarm clock was set for 0500. My body alarm clock was set to hoist me out of deep sleep and to be awake ten minutes before the alarm sounded so I could shut it off and prepare for the day without waking my wife, Lesley. In my thirteen years on the North Sea my body clock only let me down once. I slept on. The alarm clock woke her and the children. I rose to face the dawn accompanied by two vocally excited kids and an extremely grumpy bride. I never made the same mistake again. I think it's called 'aversion conditioning'.

One's body alarm clock, however, can be upstaged by a bantam cockerel. We were in the process of taking over an old farmhouse complete with fields, stables and a wooden barn. I received a phone call from my solicitor, Mr Sutherland, the semi-retired senior partner and sort of Emeritus Professor of Smith and Sutherland Advocates, whose offices were in Union Street, Aberdeen. He dealt with all my three house purchases while I was on the North Sea. I confess I grew fond of the old man.

"I can't complete Captain.' he said, 'The vendors have no given vacant possession."

This might have been bad news except that Mr. Sutherland could not suppress a chuckle.

"Why is that Mr. Sutherland?"

"It's a cockerel. They've got the hens out, but they can't get the cockerel you see. He's up one of your trees and he's no coming down".

"I don't think we should delay the transaction for that should we?". In my ignorance of poultry, I found the idea of a resident bantam cockerel quite appealing.

"Well I shouldn't need to remind you Captain, that in these parts in summer the dawn starts to break at 3.30 in the morn, and cockerels can make a terrible racket at day-break."

"I'm sure it will be alright Mr. Sutherland."

A few days later the date for moving into our new home arrived. That evening I made hot chocolate for Lesley, exhausted after a long day. The cockerel had flown down from the tree and, initially from a distance, had strutted about inspecting everything. He had delighted the children, who promptly named him 'Jake' and cut up bits of bacon rind to coax him to be friendly. This meant he was now officially a member of our family and he gave the distinct impression that he knew it.

The month was July when the days were very long and the nights very short. We went to bed as the sky started to darken. Five hours later the sky started to lighten again and Jake let rip from the top of a tree right next to our bedroom window. Lesley and I sat bolt upright in bed, hearts palpitating. But within three days our body clocks refused to hear it while we were asleep. Jake, despite his demonic crowing, could not awaken us, and I slumbered on until 0450 when my next hurdle was to switch off the alarm clock to enable Lesley and the children to sleep on.

My uniform was always laid out in the lounge. I showered and slipped into it while still waking up. While not exactly as slick as Wallace and Gromit in "The Wrong Trousers" it was nevertheless a well-rehearsed routine. It was light outside as it was still late summer and the daylight hours would stretch through to late evening. Someone once told me that in summer it was possible to stand outside in the Shetlands at midnight and still be able to read the Aberdeen Press and Journal newspaper. He didn't offer any explanation as to why anyone would actually want to do that.

After the summer Solstice and summer gave way to autumn, this day-night imbalance began to reverse itself. By mid-winter daylight would begin to fade around mid-afternoon and it would not get properly light again until well into the following morning. The summers were mild but rarely hot; the winters in Aberdeen were cold, often well below zero for weeks on end. The roads would be coated with ice as hard as iron, and one would get to know the solid ice-bumps while commuting to and from Dyce Airport. Snow was always a possibility in winter, and I thought it remarkable that although some of the crews lived an hour's journey out from the airport or more, lateness or no-shows never seemed to be a problem. I imagine we all became quite skillful at driving cars in bad conditions as well as flying helicopters, and on days off we would think nothing of chucking the skis into the car and driving up to ski the Lecht in drifting snow. This was before the arrival of four-wheel-drive cars, but we managed.

Pilots arriving in the Planning Room were given a task to fly out to support one or more offshore installations or floating structures; they then worked out the required fuel load, the minima for which were laid down in the company Operations Manual. These procedures and requirements had to be approved by the Civil Aviation Authority (CAA). The CAA was the regulator, tasked with producing safe aviation, and the procedures and requirements had the force of law.

The most numerous helicopter on the North Sea was the versatile Sikorsky S61. It was deployed on the North Sea in increasing numbers in the 1970s and achieved creditable service, serviceability, and longevity. Other helicopters came and went, but at the time it seemed that the S61 would go on forever. It was developed from the military Sikorsky H3 which morphed into several noteworthy marques including the ubiquitous naval Sea King and the HH3, which, with its rear-loading ramp and in-flight re-fueling probe was nick-named the 'Jolly Green Giant'. The S61N is a variant of the successful SH3 Sea King helicopter. The H3 and its various progeny were amphibious helicopters, capable of landing, taxiing and taking off on both land and water.

The North Sea variant did not have any such fancy name; it was simply the S61. It hefted two turbo-shaft jet engines delivering 1500 horse power each, and in the right conditions could lift up to nineteen passengers in North Sea configuration. The limit of nineteen was the maximum the CAA considered might have a reasonable chance of escape without an assisting cabin attendant in the event of a ditching. The aircraft was capable of carrying many more, and the helicopter that ferried between Penzance and the Scilly Islands, a short overwater distance, had thirty-four passenger seats.

The requirement for the minimum fuel load was calculated in accordance with a forecast issued by the Meteorological Office called a Terminal Aerodrome Forecast, or 'TAF'. These were updated every six hours, but six hours was more than enough for conditions to change significantly, rendering fuel calculations wide of the new and possibly still changing requirement. By this time the aircraft could be airborne full of passengers, still committed to the fuel reserves dictated by the original forecast, but by changing circumstances now out of date. If changing conditions implied that you could not maintain those reserves, you were supposed to divert or even turn back to base in order to maintain them. This meant that right from the start of the trip the crew had an important task, amongst all the others, of monitoring the weather conditions, constantly recalculating its implications, and making the appropriate decisions to keep the flight on the safe side of the line.

The most bizarre phenomenon was an east coast sea fret known in Aberdeen as 'The Haar'. It is produced when warmer moist air moves over the cold North Sea. The moisture in the air cools and precipitates into fog. This might not be a problem if it just sits offshore, but if the wind direction suddenly adopts an easterly component, it will just as suddenly be blown inland shrouding the countryside in thick fog. The Haar is most likely to occur between spring and autumn. The frequency is increased by sea breezes where a warm land mass causes air above it to rise, pulling in colder air from over the sea with its fog. Aberdeen Airport, Sumburgh Airport in Shetland, and Beccles Heliport in Norfolk were our major bases for North Sea helicopter operations. They were all coastal airports and therefore susceptible to suddenly 'fogging out'. This can make nonsense of a fuel calculation that did not take it into account. If the enshrouding Haar reduces the visibility below the minimum for a visual approach, a diversion to a clear airfield may be required. If it reduces the runway visual range, or cloud base, below limits for an instrument approach using an electronic approach aid such as ILS (Instrument Landing System), similarly a diversion will be required.

Cumulo-nimbus clouds presented you with lightning, accompanied by electrical activity that could throw off both your radio-compass and Decca area navigation aid. Icing, turbulence, darkness, snow, and torrential rain were ever likely with them. These giants were the hooligans of the North Sea. They had the energy to move in directions which were at variance with the prevailing wind and could form lines of thunderstorms scores of miles long and miles in depth. Well developed, they could reach up to the Tropopause at around 35,000 feet at North Sea latitudes, which meant we could not climb over them. Not even close.

Yet strangely, for all their impressive threatening, they would be handled confidently by experienced crews. The helicopter engines had heated engine air which could be switched on to provide protection against moderate levels of engine icing. The pilots were also able to measure the degree of airframe icing in flight. The S61 had rotors that comprised five long rotor blades that twisted and flexed in flight. This could look alarming when viewed with a rotor-head mounted camera, but it was effective in shedding rotor icing and keeping them ice free. In the last event it was possible to descend to 500 feet over the sea, the descent track being checked on internal radar, where the increased temperature and salt in the air would assist in getting the blades clear of ice. If the icing level was lower than this, flight over the sea was generally prohibited.

The radar equipment was important to safe flight. It could pick up the offshore installation easily because of its size, so the crew could still vector towards it even when the aircraft's area navigation system had been knocked off-line by electrical activity within the clouds. This was not an uncommon occurrence. The area navigation system, Decca, was an old hyperbolic system developed during the Second World War. There was an extensive list of conditions where it became unreliable including coast-lines, dawn, dusk, thunderstorms and especially snow. The North Sea had the lot. With the passage of time Decca was replaced by more modern and less vulnerable systems such as RNAV and GPS.

Fortunately, however, the active centres of the lines of storms also showed up clearly on the radar scopes like tiny walnut kernels. These active storm cells had to be avoided, but if you can see them on the radar scope, you can steer between them.

Many an hour was spent with the handling pilot glued to instrument flying and the non-handling pilot peering at the radar returns calling the headings: "Left five degrees. Left a further five. OK, hold that for now – we can squeeze between those two cells."

Then the target installation would slide into the top of the screen and the approach would be arranged on scope information to try to achieve a cloud break with the rig in sight, more or less in front, some miles distant. The installation was contacted by radio for deck-condition information, and details of the inbound load. The crew gave an estimated time of arrival (ETA) to ensure the deck was prepared to receive the aircraft in good time.

"Wind from port. Rig ten degrees right. Track's good."

"OK – I'm going to point at the rig and let her drift right for a left turn into wind."

"Roger. Range 20 miles".

"Initial Approach checks please."

On some days, or nights, the weather was clear, and the crew would be able to see the destination installation perhaps a hundred miles away even before they achieved cruising altitude.

When the weather closed in requiring instrument flying, the crew would typically arrange things so that the aircraft would break cloud before 500 feet above sea level and the crew could revert to visual procedures for the final approach and landing. This might involve the non-handling pilot becoming the handling pilot at the last minute if the deck was on his side with the aircraft approaching into wind. There is, to my knowledge, no common equivalent of this in anything other than rotary wing flying, and reflects the extraordinary flexibility of these aircraft, which demanded an equivalent flexibility on the part of the pilots to exploit it.

"Final checks please."

The undercarriage would start to travel down and the wheels locked with a thump. The rest of the checks were then completed for a landing and landing clearance was obtained from the installation by radio.

The offshore landing manoeuvre was obviously critical. By the time the aircraft had flown between one hundred and two hundred miles out over the North Sea, its landing weight could be expected to be lighter than on take-off by between one thousand and two thousand pounds depending on the wind strength and direction relative to the outbound track. In other words, it might be a tonne or more lighter than on take-off. The aim was to maintain a flight path during the landing that kept the power demand low enough so that flight could be continued in the event of loss of one of the engines during the landing. In the event of a decision to divert instead, the overshoot and climb-away should also be possible on one engine. So, the approach would usually be flown to close on the helideck in a shallow descent in a gentle deceleration to try to keep the power demand low enough to execute these manoeuvres in the event of the loss of an engine. Into wind, in turbulence-free air, it was usually achievable; but if there was turbulence through a structure on the installation, or the into wind heading put the helideck in an awkward approach position, this was not always possible.

The aircraft was descended into the ground cushion, then lowered onto the deck. A thumbs-up indicated to the Deck Landing Officer that he was cleared to approach within the disc area. He would open the external door hatch, which, when lowered, presented a set of steps for disembarking passengers. During the outbound leg the non-handling pilot would carry out a series of performance and weight and balance calculations as well as calculating the required inbound fuel load. This latter was dependent on weather conditions. The inbound passengers would then board the aircraft and seat themselves according to the weight and balance plan. At the same time as all this activity was going on the aircraft remained running and was being refuelled.

Eventually, take-off checks complete, a radio call made obtaining departure clearance, the helicopter is brought to the hover, paused for more checks, then power applied. The aircraft rises from the hover, nose goes down, and she picks up forward speed into the climb. Today the cloud base is at 1,000 feet, and as the handling pilot is electing to cruise at 2,500 feet, the entire transit will be in cloud and on instruments. The departure radio call is transmitted, which is in effect a radio flight plan giving an estimate for example to the Alpha Delta November (Aberdeen) radio beacon so that Aberdeen Air Traffic (ATC) can control the phasing of inbound aircraft, including fixed wing airliners from Heathrow and Gatwick. There was a lot of traffic; Aberdeen was the oil capital of Europe after all.

Then comes the quiet bit. The non-handling pilot listens to the weather reports at destination and alternate airfields. He monitors the fuel reserves and groundspeed continually. He plots and records any wind vector changes and calculates what effect this could have on the flight. Everything is recorded in the flight log with a new line entry every ten minutes or so. It is important to detect any change in flight conditions that might make a re-plan necessary. A new plan might be made and then just set aside in readiness, but the work has been done already. Apart from at Christmas, helicopter pilots do not like surprises.

Meanwhile, the handling pilot concentrates on accurate instrument flying, occasionally sipping coffee. In those days, cigarettes could be smoked.

Eventually they coast in, although the coast cannot be seen due to cloud. Air Traffic Control steers them on a heading which will intercept the Instrument Landing System (ILS) beams. The ILS needles come alive, and the S61 commences its descent and approach entirely on the track and glide path information provided by them, at an airspeed of 100 knots.

"Undercarriage down and locked, checks complete for landing".

"Golf India Delta you are cleared to land runway One Seven."

"Golf India Delta Roger. Clear to land One Seven."

The non-handling pilot places a hand on both throttles, known as Speed Select Levers in the S61, ready to deliver full power in the event of a go-around. The altimeters are checked once again for the correct setting. The aircraft may be descended to 200 feet above ground level on this kind of approach and, if the runway lights are visible by then, landed. If there is no visual contact it must carry out a go-around procedure, still on instruments. It may attempt a second approach but, if this is not successful, must divert to an alternate airfield where the weather is good enough for a safe landing to be made.

"Passing 1,000 feet no contact,"

"Roger."

At 700 feet – "Just starting to get the lights".

At 400 feet – "Airfield in sight – good visual. Decide."

The handling pilot glances up from the instrument panel, acquires the runway with its lights, and says:

"Landing."

He runs the aircraft onto the runway without bringing her to a hover and ground taxies back into the dispersal to minimise down-wash. Brakes on, thumbs up, chocks in, the S61 engines are shut down and the rotor brake applied.

The door is opened and nineteen rig-workers smelling strongly of shampoo and aftershave deplane. They have been cooped up offshore for a fortnight and they are in a hurry to get back home. They look like men who definitely have something on their minds.

For the pilots there is no hurry. They have already passed the next fuel load to British Airways Helicopters Operations by radio. Just time to go for a pee, which was a bit involved when wearing a rubber immersion suit, then walk back out and do it all over again. Or something like it. If the flying programme is running late however, the aircraft might be kept running, including during a change of crew if required. These procedures were quite straightforward on a benign day, but unfortunately there were days that were not benign, far from it. In conditions of strong and gusting wind for example, it might be necessary to start engines and rotors inside a hangar to prevent the blades flapping down and hitting the tail at low rotor speeds. That would definitely ruin your day.

At the end of flying it was not unusual for pilots to adjourn to the Dyce Skean Dhu Hotel bar. British Airways pilots were not supposed to be seen drinking beer in uniform so we used to take off our jackets, remove our rank bars from shirt epaulettes, and the hotel would suddenly be filled by men in white shirts, black trousers and ties, ruminating on the day's events and sharing the latest 'gen'. It was an enjoyable way to wind down after a day in the cockpit, cracking jokes and taking the mickey. It cemented some strong friendships, many of which have lasted to this day.

Chapter Nine

When Things Go Wrong

Captain Ian Recton

Helicopters are complex machines, containing many rotating parts. They are installed in the engines, in the gear boxes connecting the drives to the main and tail rotor. Pitch operating arms, links and hydraulic jacks, pipelines for fuel and hydraulics, and so on. Every part in this myriad of wheels, teeth, bearings, and turbine blades is finely machined and assembled to exact measurements with little tolerance and wear allowed. Virtually every part therefore is subject to fatigue and wear. They need to be replaced, preferably before they break! Thus, the manufacturer places a design life on all parts. A rigorous test schedule is followed to achieve final approval and certification of the helicopter. In addition, all crew and safety equipment requirements, operating weather limits, both under visual and instrument rules, are established. All the helicopters in use on the North Sea are certified as suitable for their individual role, which is mainly the carriage of personnel over the sea to oil and gas platforms, in visual and instrument conditions. Some helicopters are cleared to operate in 'light icing conditions'. The Sikorsky S61N, the early North Sea workhorse, was so cleared.

The human story then, behind a helicopter coming into service embraces many people with a variety of knowledge and specialist skills. The scope for error is vast but it is recognised and understood. Manufacturers have checks and balances in place to ensure that all parts will function correctly without failure for as long as expected by the design and testing process. Systemic quality control at all stages, so to speak. Regulators and Operators are required to set up procedures and training programmes for the crews, to cover all flight aspects expected to be encountered in the environment of operation, including emergency procedures. So, what can possibly go wrong?

Virtually every incident narrated in this chapter has a 'human error' link, somewhere in its cause. Yet most crews would be horrified to think they might have been a part of the chain, even inadvertently. But we all make mistakes, especially under pressure. Most pilots facing a sudden unexpected occurrence during flight will probably admit, after the initial 'spontaneous expletive' that they thought they might have done something wrong Then, their training and procedures 'kicked in' allowing a calmer appraisal to take place. The maxim was 'Fly First'.

Certainly, all are very aware of the complex nature of these machines operating in sometimes marginal and hostile conditions. After each major incident or accident, the Air Accident Investigation Branch (AAIB) is charged with finding the cause. The crew are usually suspended from flying duties while the inquiry proceeds. These inquiries are to be impartial and with the purpose of making recommendations to improve maintenance, design or operating procedures, so that the CEO can say, "procedures have been put in place so that this will not happen again". And so, humans learn, maybe!

As a result, over the years, there have been many improvements in equipment and training for both crews and passengers for the underwater escape and survival aspects. The 'dunkers' and equipment at the Robert Gordon Institute were excellent, albeit they were slow in coming. The 'in service' helicopters are improved through modification programmes. Helicopter flight simulators were introduced to improve all aspects of training particularly for the in-flight emergency actions. New helicopter types are designed using lighter and more effective materials as new technologies allow and start to come into service.

There is a sad truth though. It usually took accident fatalities to spur action at Regulator and Department of Transport level, in order that all operators introduce the same improvements across the board.

A helicopter operator may be disinclined unilaterally to introduce expensive safety measures at the cost of payload if others refuse because this might involve incurring commercial disadvantage. This is especially relevant when the client corporate policy is deliberately to fine tune contracts to keep the helicopter operators grateful and insecure. They played the competition just enough to keep the price minimal but not enough to cause too many operators to go out of business! The industry corporates should have a responsibility to their skilled workforces to enhance safety. This then, was the environment for helicopter services in support of the oil and gas industry over the North Sea.

As young trainee pilots in the RAF we were taken out to Bridlington harbour through a snow-covered Yorkshire landscape on a February morning. We boarded the RAF launch and were told to change into our swimming costumes, a pair of denims to simulate our flight suits and a lifejacket. Meanwhile the launch headed out to sea. We could not see the land. We were given a single seat dinghy pack which was the one fitted to our training aircraft, the Jet Provost. Each one of us in turn, threw the pack into the water holding onto the lanyard and followed it into the sea. It was imperative to inflate and board the dinghy and get the canopy around you quickly. Within a few minutes, with the floor and canopy inflated, and after baling out the water, it was 'snug' in the dinghy. Later, the rescue helicopter arrived overhead. When the helicopter winchman came down on the winch cable to attach the lifting strop, the downdraught made it very cold as one by one we were dragged back to the launch. This training, along with underwater escape training during our helicopter conversion phase, made the message very clear! Know your equipment and how to use it. RN crews were no doubt even more aware of the potential dangers of flying over the sea.

In my own case, not one but two incidents resulted in water landings. I was not in command but felt the pressure just as keenly as the commanders. Both inquiries however were thorough and made recommendations that were quickly put into action.

The first one, which occurred in S61 G-BEID, was avoidable. If we as the crew had all the knowledge the manufacturer only later disclosed with regard to the main rotor gearbox capabilities after its cooling system stops functioning; and had an oil temperature gauge been fitted calibrated to cover the entire temperature range possible, there would have been no incident. No such information was included in the technical manuals or emergency training.

After eight years commercial flying with seven years on off-shore helicopters I returned to a second RAF career flying rotary and fixed wing aircraft until retirement.

Most of the stories related here are written by the commander involved. The justification for decisions made are corroborated by Air Accident Investigation reports, their own notes and the recollection of the other crew members. Sometimes what happened during a rescue phase can seem farcical and incompetent especially when it comes to launching and boarding multi seat life rafts in even a small swell. Imagine for a moment, being in a bouncy castle floating on water. Your legs just don't work very well! If a flavour of the 'crew room' or 'bar chat bravado' is detected it should be forgiven. Underlying each narrative, is the uneasy feeling that given different circumstances things might have been much worse. Had it been at night, or in a sea rough enough to turn the aircraft upside down on touchdown; or if the 'break up' of the gearbox component had been completely uncontained as happened to a BV 234 LR Chinook with the loss of forty-two out of forty-four souls on board, this might have been the result.

Tragically this was the case for some of our then, young colleagues. They did not return home to their families that day. They are not here to write their story. Tragically too this was the case for the men and women who were their passengers.

So, "There but for the Grace of God, go I".

Chapter Ten

Close Shaves 1

Captain Tony Dando

August 14 1985 should have been my last day on this earth. With my co-pilot Ian Maryan we had just completed a 3-hour 45-minute trip to the Aladdin rig and back for BP in Bell 214ST G-BKFN and were scheduled to immediately do another one to the Glomar Biscay II for Shell. I still have the Cockpit Voice Recorder (CVR) tape which retained the last thirty minutes of flight. In those days we used to be marshalled onto our parking spot by our delightful ground hostesses in their British Caledonian Helicopters (BCHL) tartan kilts. The first words on the CVR as we taxied in from the first flight are from Ian 'Let's pull a bit of pitch and see if we can make Holly's kilt fly'.

We refuelled with the rotors turning, loaded our passengers, fifteen men and one woman, and took off with Ian flying the helicopter and me looking after the radios. As we crossed the coastline, level at our cruising altitude of 3,000 feet, there was a hell of a bang and the helicopter started vibrating so much that I couldn't see the instruments, nor could I easily control my arms in order to lock my harness. Ian immediately put the helicopter into autorotation and put out a Mayday call which was garbled as the vibrations distorted his voice. He had said we were going to land on the beach. Once I had my harness locked, I took control of the helicopter and asked him to retransmit the Mayday as I intended going for a field next to the main Aberdeen to Ellon Road so that emergency services could get to us easily.

Control was difficult as there were feedback forces which were intermittently defeating the hydraulic systems and after about 75 seconds or so we landed downwind in a field near the village of Balmedie, still doing 60 knots as I couldn't slow the helicopter down any more or turn into wind. Some passengers then opened the sliding doors and were starting to bail out as we hurtled along the ground but the helicopter was hopping from one main wheel to the other with the vibration and they could well have been struck by the main rotor blades. We screamed at them to stay inside the helicopter and eventually we came to a stop, shut down the engines and electrics and evacuated everyone forward of the aircraft and counted heads.

A few minutes later I saw a Bristow Super Puma helicopter coming down the coast looking for us so I turned the batteries back on so I could talk to him and advise there were no injuries. At this point Ian made the second of his notable pronouncements that day when in an attempt to lighten the mood as everyone was in shock and he can be heard on the CVR shouting "Anyone need a clean pair of underpants?".

The Super Puma came to a hover in the field and the captain, Pete Beglan, radioed that he had six seats available if any of my passengers wanted a lift back to the airport. Looking around at them, some lying on the ground in shock, I declined that offer.

Two fire engines and the police arrived fairly quickly but fortunately were not needed. I presume ambulances arrived as well but I can't recall that. Ian and I did our best to comfort those passengers worst affected by shock until the arrival of a coach sent by our company to return them to the airport.

The two of us stayed on site until our engineers arrived and we handed things over to them. Ian and I were taken back to our offices where we were led into the managing director's office where we relayed details of the incident to him. I think it was at this point, some two hours after it happened that we both began to feel the effects of shock. The MD gave us a couple of large shots of brandy each and a while later he arranged that we were taken to see the local Civil Aviation Authority Authorised Medical Examiner to get checked over. I've never been sure of the wisdom of that after a large brandy! Apart from the implications of driving after we had the alcohol, neither of us felt like doing that anyway so cars and drivers were arranged to take us home.

The Air Accident Investigation Board (AAIB) Investigators arrived in Aberdeen the next day and Ian and I were interviewed. In due course an AAIB Bulletin was issued detailing the findings of the Board.

Some months later the managing director of the British Caledonian Group came from Headquarters at Gatwick Airport to Aberdeen to make awards to the two of us and pass on the Group's thanks to for how things were handled during and after the incident. In spite of my protestations, I was then taken to the Grampian TV studios to be interviewed during the evening's news programme – I found that almost as nerve wracking as the incident itself!

We were very lucky as had the emergency had happened a minute later we would have had to ditch in the sea and in view of the control difficulties we experienced it would likely not have been successful. When the main rotor mast was taken out of the helicopter and rolled on a bench it was found to be curved because of the vibration forces. The opinion of the manufacturer was that it probably would not have lasted much longer before breaking. The cause of the emergency was the fracture due to internal corrosion of one of the two drag braces on the main rotor. The following year this same helicopter was successfully ditched in the sea seventeen miles off Fraserburgh because of control problems – basically the collective lever control run integrity was breached and no collective pitch control was available. The co-pilot was once again Ian Maryan. The helicopter was recovered from the sea, returned to service after repairs and it continued flying on offshore exploration and production related tasks in the North Sea until the type was withdrawn in 2007. G-BKFN is now thirty-eight years old and still flying (2020) for another operator in the wilds of northern Canada.

In 2015, some thirty years after the incident, an ex-Royal Navy pilot friend of mine asked if he could listen to the CVR tape of the incident. As soon as the emergency occurred on the tape I had to leave the room. Emotion got the better of me and I couldn't listen to it. After all the intervening years the depth of that reaction surprised me.

Chapter Eleven

Close Shaves 2:
The Importance of Crew Teamwork

Captain Peter Saxton

I t's something of an irony that of all the hundreds of flights you undertake in a flying career, few are particularly memorable because most go well. The memorable ones are usually those where something *un*usual occurs, and by that criterion there is nothing more memorable than a life-threatening incident.

On 20 May 1987 I was Commander of G-BKZH, a Super Puma AS332L helicopter. I elected to be the handling pilot on the outbound trip to the Sedneth 701 from Aberdeen with seventeen passengers on board. The Sedneth 701 was a semi-submersible rig operating 35 miles northeast of Unst, in the northern Shetlands. Memories of that flight had become hazy but re-reading the internal company report and the Air Accidents Investigation Board (AAIB) report after so long feels almost like living it again. Not altogether pleasant.

There are some bits in the reports that still make me swallow. We were in cloud, instrument flying, just coming abeam Unst, our track northeast around forty miles offshore. There was a sudden bang. The aircraft vibrated violently and pitched up. Tail Rotor failure?! Normal instrument attitude reference – the Attitude Director Indicators or ADIs – became very blurred due to the vibration. That was bad enough but what made my blood run cold was the rush of suspicion that both main ADIs had become unreliable. In cloud we were reliant on them to control the aircraft. The real peril lay in the fact that *both* instruments seemed to be indicating we were in a pitched up and rolled attitude; only the standby Attitude Indicator

(AI) showed us pitched up and straight. A cross-check showed other instruments were consistent with the standby AI so I chose to believe that. I carried out a recovery-from-unusual-attitude using this instrument, which successfully restored straight and level flight; but in those few moments everything could have gone disastrously wrong.

It was not a lucky day, but I did have one ace card – my co-pilot, Captain Tony Wickes. Tony was one of the most experienced Super Puma pilots on the North Sea and had a long history with the Puma in its various versions. He had been one of the team managing the introduction of the aircraft into operation with the company. He was a cool, left-brain sort of flyer, and come the day you have to handle a pig's breakfast like a tail rotor failure in cloud over the sea, you couldn't have a better pilot sitting alongside you.

The aircraft was still flying, but for how long? We discussed the situation, the implications, and made a plan. I had immediately adopted the Tail Rotor Failure emergency procedure, and from there on we continued to fly the aircraft in accordance with those. Tony double-checked completion of the emergency check lists and transmitted a Mayday call to Shetland Radar as calmly as if he was doing a practice in the simulator. The AAIB report concluded that adoption of the Tail Rotor Failure procedure, with the consequent reduction in speed and torque, had stopped the tail gearbox from coming off completely. Another retrospective swallow.

I had turned towards the nearest diversion – Unst airport now some 35 nautical miles distant, but there was a big chance we wouldn't make it. If the vibration got any worse, we would have to ditch. Tony therefore briefed the passengers for a ditching in the North Sea. Then he discovered that the cabin intercom had failed due to the high level of vibration, so he re-briefed them using hand signs. I didn't detect an ounce of emotion in Tony – he just calmly got on with the day-job. Two search and rescue helicopters were vectored towards us.

Eventually we descended clear of cloud into visual flying conditions and looked at the sea; in those big waves, ditching looked a very unattractive option. A capsize had to be considered likely, and the Super Puma exits would not jettison if the aircraft inverted, trapping the passengers upside down inside a sinking aircraft. Out of the question. We had to keep flying as long as we could.

We descended further in case a ditching became unavoidable, but began picking up turbulence, which yawed the aircraft – absolutely the last thing we needed with a severely damaged tail rotor. We let her drift upwards again until things smoothed out. Our conclusion remained that our best hope was to get to the runway on Unst and carry out a running landing. This would enable us to use the directional stability provided by the tail fin to keep us straight – we had to resist any temptation to use the tail rotor to control yaw on the approach and landing.

Unst Island, and then the airfield runway eventually came into sight. We were cleared to land on runway 30. I set up the approach for a running landing in accordance with the Tail Rotor Failure drill – low collective torque to maintain 60 knots and 500 ft/min descent. The drill said that the wind should be slightly from the right for this manoeuvre, the sort of instruction that made us chuckle cynically in the crew-room. How likely was that on the average day? I expected the aircraft nose to be crabbed off the aircraft's track, but this would not do. If she touched down from a running landing insufficiently aligned, she could roll over; and when a chopper rolls over all hell breaks loose. We were considering how to deal with this when we saw that it might not be necessary. There was indeed the much – desired crosswind slightly from the right, which weather-vaned the aircraft nose, aligning us nearly perfectly down the runway. We touched down with a shimmy into an otherwise uneventful roll out. Never were two gas turbines shut down so rapidly. The whole thing had taken less than twenty-five minutes. Somehow, it seemed longer.

The rest of the day was spent in a bit of a daze. The excitement calmed down and I had time to reflect on the fact that for nineteen people the day might have ended very differently. I don't remember anything of the journey back to Aberdeen. I do remember an engineer telling me that he reckoned we only had a few minutes flying time left before the aircraft came apart; and I do remember thinking "A few minutes left is just fine by me".

The aftermath seemed to me to have been unbalanced in one important respect. There were compliments – lots of "cool professionalism" and so on – a Guild of Air Pilots Award even. But the credits were over-focused on me as the Commander. While the buck stops with the Commander, that is by no means the whole story. It was a crew effort. We and the passengers could not have walked away from something as dangerous as that unless Tony and I had been trained to work together, hand in glove, as a single unit. Subsequently, during my years as a Senior Manager with British Airways I was pleased to note a greater tendency to recognize the whole crew when the chips were down and they managed it. It takes the whole crew working together.

Chapter Twelve

Rescue Operations:
The Vee Skerries Rescue 9th September 1977

Captain Tony Buckley

In the early days of offshore helicopter operations out of the Sumburgh airfield in Shetland, the oil companies and the helicopter operators realised just how vulnerable the helicopters, their crews and their passengers were in the event of any emergency which necessitated a ditching in the Northern North Sea. The nearest SAR helicopter was based at RAF Lossiemouth which was 2 to 3 hours flying time from Shetland plus further time flying from there to the scene of the event, which could be another couple of hours.

British Airways Helicopters' main client, Shell, agreed to fund the flying required for crew training in order to create a form of "self-help" rescue capability. The S61N helicopter could readily be fitted with a hydraulically powered winch, and ex-service personnel with experience in helicopter winching operations volunteered for some fairly basic training. As I had just recently left the RAF where my last posting was as an instructor at the Search and Rescue Training Unit at RAF Valley I agreed to carry out the pilot training with the help of an ex-Navy winch operator, Brian Johnson. I also provided rudimentary training for the volunteers who agreed to act as winchmen and hang on the end of the winch cable. This was designed to enable them to control their "flight" through the air and how to place survivors into the rescue strop both on land and in the water. One of these volunteers was an ex-Guards Regiment Major, Captain Alasdair Campbell.

Alasdair had only had a couple of training exercises as winchman (the impossibly brave crew who jump out and save lives dangling on a steel cable a hundred feet below a hovering helicopter at night in a storm) when he volunteered to do it with Captain George Bain. First Officer Campbell Bosanquet, and expert Winch Operator Brian Johnson, were available when the emergency call-out came on the night of the 9th December 1977.

A Shetland fishing trawler had reported running aground on the Vee Skerries rocks off the North West coast of the Shetland Islands. The weather was atrocious, with gale force winds, heavy rain causing poor forward visibility, and low cloud base. The helicopter left the base at Sumburgh and flew low-level around the west coast into the area of the Skerrie rocks. The windscreen wipers were batting frantically. They searched the area for a long time without seeing anything of the trawler. They searched just above mountainous waves, having only the landing lights of the helicopter for illumination. They were about to give up the search when Campbell Bosanquet said that he could smell diesel fumes.

Captain Bain, flying on instruments at 200 feet, banked the S61 into wind and slowly crept forward until their lights lit up the wrecked boat on the rocks. They then came to the hover in a gale-force wind, and as the best rescue position was from port, Campbell Bosanquet flew the rescue hover. They winched off all 8 crew members. During the winching, Captain Alasdair Campbell, a pilot but a volunteer emergency Winch-Man, was swung and hit against a mast and entangled in rigging. Severely injured, hanging 50 feet below the rescue helicopter, he continued the rescue. The last of the crew, the Master of the ship, was reluctant to leave and had to be "persuaded" by a thump from Alasdair.

No ships' crew had ever survived a wreck on the Vee Skerries. The Shetlanders were most appreciative of the efforts of the rescuers and of the presence of the helicopter companies on the island. It was a pleasure to shop in Lerwick wearing a BRITISH AIRWAYS

HELICOPTERS waterproof. People would abandon the fruit and veg. to shake your hand.

Captain George Bain and Captain Alasdair Campbell were awarded The Queen's Gallantry Medals. The other crew members, First Officer Campbell Bosanquet; and crewman Brian Johnson, were awarded Queen's Commendations for Valuable Service In The Air.

Brave men All! Alas, all no longer with us.

Chapter Thirteen

The Finneagle Rescue: October 1980

Squadron Leader William Campbell AFC

At 8.27pm on 1st October 1980 a distress message on 500 kilohertz triggered the Auto Alarm signal at BT's Wick Coastal Radio Station: "This is Motor Ship Finneagle in position 59°15'N 04°11'W, Fire on board". What followed for members of 202 Squadron's SAR Sea King Flight at RAF Lossiemouth and one of the station's Medical Officers was a night of unforgettable experiences.

The Swedish Marine Accident Report begins with the initial loading of the 14,497-tonne deadweight Swedish roll-on/roll-off vessel in Vera Cruz, Mexico on 15 September. Further loading took place in Houston, Mobile and New Orleans from where Finneagle departed on 21 September bound for Wallhamn, 30 miles north of Gothenburg, Sweden. She was to follow a course that would take her north of Rockall and through the Pentland Firth, keeping her south of 2 low-pressure areas where the predicted maximum wave heights were forecast to increase to over 25 feet. After passing Rockall, wind and sea had increased in strength and by midday on 1 October the Captain estimated the wind to have reached 10-12 on the Beaufort Scale (10 Storm, 11 Severe Storm, 12 Hurricane), with a following sea estimated to have reached a height of 40 feet.

There was a significant load of chemical containers in the cargo, carrying large and small tanks, drums, tins and cylinders. Some, listed as toxic or corrosive or highly flammable liquids and gases, were classified as dangerous cargo. Just to add to the cocktail were paints, varnishes, adhesives, petroleum products and alcohol including bottled whisky. Despite efforts to secure the cargo, four units, including a tank-container full of trimethyl phosphite, had broken their fastenings and slid against empty refrigerator trailers. A strange smell was noticed but although the tank-container had received damage to its thick insulation it was impossible to see any damage to the tank itself. On top of this had been stowed a container with drums of synthetic rubber solution which had also been damaged, allowing the rubber solution to run out. After further work, by 5pm the cargo was considered provisionally secured.

At 7pm the captain altered course to avoid the Pentland Firth and transit north of the Orkney Islands. Between 7.30 and 8pm the vessel made several violent lurches as a result of which the trimethyl phosphite container came adrift again. This time the crew could not secure it. While the crew were there the container bumped repeatedly against a refrigerator trailer on the starboard side and at 8.20pm fire broke out. According to the second mate white smoke began to rise and then a ball of yellow-orange fire appeared. Trimethyl phosphite reacts violently with acid with a marked increase in temperature. The refrigerator trailers were all equipped with charged batteries and everything points to these being knocked off their mountings allowing dilute sulphuric acid to leak and react with the trimethyl phosphite.

Those crewmembers who were 'tween decks were forced to leave quickly. The fire, which spread fiercely resulting in the development of great heat, set off the fire alarm. The released heat led to the heating up of the weather deck above (the uncovered part of the upper deck) and inflammable gases developed leading to an explosion. Shortly afterwards there was a further violent explosion. Some of the force of this was dissipated by a 40-tonne container lorry parked on the lift, which was blown from the lower deck to the roof of 'tween decks and fell back. Two ventilators with their 4-tonne impeller motors were blown clean out of the ship. The first distress message was sent at 8.27pm.

The subsequent rapid spread of the fire indicates that after it had started the heat caused the trimethyl phosphite to vaporise. The swift development of heat led to the vaporisation of different substances. These gases were later to ignite and explode at several points on the vessel. The rubber solution and other spilled liquids caused the fire to spread to the decks below and ignite among other things the foam plastic insulation on the refrigerator trailers considerably stimulating the fire and leading to the development of great quantities of smoke and noxious substances.

At 8.55pm the electrics failed and the main engine stopped leaving the ship rolling violently in a 'thwartships sea with a list of 45°. Within 15-20 minutes the first engineer succeeded in restarting the engine but only at about half speed. Steering was also restored but with no rudder position indication. At 9.30pm the firefighting sprinkler system had to be stopped as the 300 tons of water used threatened to capsize the vessel which was listing 45-55°. By 10.30pm fire had spread to the weather deck where it became raging. The after part of the ship had to be evacuated because of dense smoke and gases and the crew were finally forced to move to the wing bridges and the top bridge above the wheelhouse. Preparations were made to abandon ship but the captain decided that sea conditions made this impossible. At 11pm even the radio room, which opens directly into the wheelhouse, was evacuated.

Shortly afterwards at 11.15pm the first Rescue Helicopter, Rescue 37, arrived on scene, knowing little more than that there had been a 'fire on board'. At 8.36pm the ship's initial distress message had been relayed to Orkney Coastguard at Kirkwall who at 8.45pm scrambled the Sumburgh S-61 helicopter. At 9pm the RAF Rescue Co-ordination Centre (RCC) at Pitreavie Castle in Fife scrambled the Kinloss SAR Nimrod, an RAF long-range maritime patrol aircraft and rang Lossiemouth. Flight Lieutenant Jim Gatherer's rescue helicopter got airborne at 9.20pm, callsign Rescue 37, estimating the ship at 10.40pm. Rescue 17, the Sumburgh S-61, was estimating airborne at 9.30 with 90 minutes transit. The Nimrod, callsign Rescue 51 got airborne at 9.35pm and at 10pm located the ship.

I had been on duty since 8am acting as the flight's response cell for Lossiemouth's Tactical Evaluation Exercise (TACEVAL) to keep the duty crew free of disruption. After Rescue 37's departure I started thinking about how this operation was going to pan out. I didn't know conditions on scene but the meteorological forecast was giving a surface wind of 30-40 knots gusting 50-60, so the sea state could be imagined. I thought that we should find some off-duty aircrew and get another aircraft with full fuel and six hours endurance up there to complete the job if the scrambled aircraft ran out of fuel. I put my concerns to the RCC Controller and at 10.10pm RCC asked us to generate a second crew. We found a co-pilot, young first-tourist Flight Lieutenant Lieutenant Dave Simpson and winchman Sargent Rick Bragg. Meanwhile the estimated times of arrivals of the helicopters went further back, Rescue 37 to 11.20pm and Rescue 17, who had had a delayed departure, was estimating 11.45pm. I felt it was becoming more likely that the Rescue Co-ordination Centre were going to have to use us, but we didn't have a Captain. No Captain, no flight. Our last chance was Flight Lieutenant Mike Lakey who was away on leave of absence. Was he back? He had flown to London that day for a press conference announcing an award to a Boulmer crew for the Alexander Kielland rescue operation. Mike had just got home when I rang him at 10.20pm. Ten minutes later RCC asked us to launch a rescue helicopter. At 10.50pm Flight Lieutenant Lakey and his crew were airborne en route, with a fifth crewmember, one of the station medical officers, Squadron Leader Hamish Grant.

They stayed low, in the relatively sheltered Moray Firth, but as they passed John O'Groats they hit a 50-knot headwind. At 11.40pm they got a surprise when they heard Rescue 37 was leaving the scene to refuel at Kirkwall in the Orkney Islands having been unable to carry out winching rescue. Flight Sergeant Ron Webb, Rescue 37's Radar/Winch Operator, described to me how despondent the ship's Captain had been on the radio when they told him they were departing,

The Captain "Can you at least take the women and children?" he pleaded.

Captain –

"If we could get them off, we could get all of you off."

They were on scene trying to save lives against a 52-foot whippy signals mast had stood on the corner of the only area available for winching on the entire ship. Frustrated they certainly were, with the Captain having the agony of having to consider risking the life of his Sergeant Winchman.

But –

They were critical in preparing the way for the following rescue helicopters, thundering towards them in the storm.

The helicopter Captain, sitting in the hover 50 feet above the ship, battered by the gale, holding the ship in his landing lights, told the ship's crew to dismantle the array of masts dotted around the forward superstructure. He was running out of fuel. The signal mast in particular had to be destroyed and out of the way before the Royal Air Force arrived.

The RAF pilots picked up the ship on radar at 30 miles. One of the crew, David, a science graduate, recommended we turn left after recognising some nasty chemical fumes emanating from it. They arrived at 0.25am to be greeted by a fantastic sight. This 600 foot long, 15000-tonne ship, was pounding along, every few seconds the bow crashing into huge waves, the stern rising and falling 100 feet, rudder and propeller frequently exposed. From every aperture from bow to stern dense black smoke was billowing and midships a fire was raging on the open deck. The rear superstructure was almost totally obscured by smoke, but the most horrific sight was up front. A large block shaped forward superstructure topped off by a prominent radar mast sat just aft of a very short bow. Below them in the darkness, was the S61 rescue helicopter, in the hover above the ship.

The Sumburgh S-61 was bucking around with 65 foot of winch wire and rescue strops flailing in the turbulence. They had been trying for 40 minutes to get the strops to the crew and we watched their valiant efforts for another 10 minutes before they conceded defeat and flew off to refuel at Kirkwall, the trademark red dayglow chevrons on the hull of the Bristows' aircraft reflecting the glow of the flames as it towered away.

The time was 0.38am, more than four hours from the start of the incident, and we who had got airborne as a backup aircraft now found ourselves in the hot seat. Although we had had a good look at the ship already, we did a quick circuit to check all the hazards and it was obvious that there was only one winching area and that was where the crew, now confirmed as 22, were mustered, on the top bridge above the wheelhouse.

The light-coloured area in the aerial photograph was the roof of the Navigation Deck which housed the wheelhouse, radio room, captain's offices and pilot's room. The forward bulwark above the wheelhouse windows provided some shelter and a waist-high guard-rail bounded the rest of the perimeter. Flanking this area on either side was a yellow semi-opaque roof over an open deck area. On the 44-foot mast were mounted two radar scanners and an array of lighting gantries. Two tall whip aerials were mounted on the forward bulwark behind which some of the crew were sheltering under space blankets. Others were waiting between the mast and the guard-rail on the port side and we targeted them for the first lift.

Our instruments indicated a wind of 50 knots gusting 60-70 and waves 40-50 feet high. We caught glimpses of the helmsman spinning the wheel trying to keep the bow head into wind and sea. He had no rudder position indicator due to fire damage, so the course was erratic and the ship, being pounded by waves from either flank, was rolling 15-20 degrees either way. The biggest problem, however, was the pitching. The bow would be lifted by a wave then as the wave passed along the vessel to midships the bulbous bow would topple into the next trough before smashing into another wave. Our Doppler showed that the impact reduced the ship's speed instantly from 12 knots to 4 knots before the bulbous bow punched out of the back of the wave, whereupon the ship surged forward and accelerated back to 12 knots. As the ship rose on the wave the bow lifted an enormous chunk of water, possibly 20 feet deep, which hung momentarily on the bow before thumping into the bridge in a cloud of spray then cascading over the sides of the bow like a giant emptying a bucket. This process was repeated every 7 seconds or so, and every seventh wave was bigger than the others.

It's always preferable to get the winchman on to the deck to supervise the recovery of survivors so we decided to try as Rick, the most gutsy winchman I've ever flown with, was willing. Following my directions, Mike had to move right and follow the ship's gyrations to try to get Rick to the exact point just to the left of the mast. Within seconds the impact of the coarse control inputs Mike was having to make began a swing and then as we moved closer to the ship Rick was hit by invisible waves of air which were gushing around the superstructure. Rick was soon in a huge anti-clockwise spin, disappearing round the front of the helicopter and reappearing several seconds later behind the tail. This was madness, so we moved left, damped out the swing and brought a grateful Rick back to the cabin.

We would now have to resort to our only alternative, using our Hi-line equipment to lower two rescue strops to the deck, leaving the crew to use their initiative to get safely into the strops and indicate to us that they were ready to be winched up. We could have three attempts with our Hi-line sets, each 150 feet of braided nylon cord and diver's weights with a nylon weak link connecting to the winch hook.

Coming in from the side of the ship trailing the Hi-line was impossible due to the turbulence so we were forced to trail it from ahead of the ship. Even here the line was snaking in all directions and the one kilogramme weight was floating like a feather on the airflow. Frequently the aircraft and the ship got a bit close and for safety we stopped and joined two Hi-lines together to increase the spacing and put a total of 7 kg on the line. This gave us comfortable clearance, but the weight was still flying beautifully. It was right over the outstretched hands of the crew for ages, but we just couldn't get it to drop. Suddenly Rick shouted, "They've got it!" (followed by a big cheer from the rest of us). The weight had crashed to the deck at the rear of the top bridge with the line draped over the mast. The top bridge is known to mariners as the 'Monkey Island' and it was with the alacrity of a monkey that one of the crew shinned up the mast and released the line. Game on!

We backed off and came to the hover alongside the aft corner of the top bridge. The Hi-line was now being hauled into a scrum of people to the left of the mast. There was no lighting apart from our helicopter lights and it was impossible to see what was going on. After a few seconds someone on the deck made a rotating motion with a torch which we took to mean ready for winching. I couldn't make out who was in the strops as I gave Mike instructions to move forward and right 25 yards for the lift. All went well until we were within a couple of yards of the pickup point. We didn't know it but a rogue wave had come along, the ship had dived into a deeper trough, been slowed more severely and been lifted higher than even a seventh wave had done. I sensed that Mike had lost visual contact with the ship. The result was the mast was rearing up and rolling towards us and my brain computed a collision. Regardless of what's on the wire, heartless though that may sound, aircraft safety always comes first, and I had no option but to give Mike the emergency climb command, "UP! UP! UP!". We were still closing with the mast so I continued to shout, raising my voice and increasing the pitch until my voice broke on the seventh "UP!". What happened in the next 2 seconds is a terrible memory. I looked down the slack cable to see with horror that the mast had rolled across it. Beyond the mast I could see the scrum of people but between them and us were the two scanners and the lighting gantries. I remember the thoughts flashing through my mind. "Can I stop Mike from climbing? No! They're going to be shredded! What are my next words going to be!". Well, with indescribable relief, I was able to say the normal "Clear of the deck, clear left, survivors on the hook", because a split second before we started climbing away, the ship lurched to starboard and the mast rolled clear of the cable. The survivors in the strops were wrenched off the deck (as Mike was later to say "like a Saturn Five Rocket!") and sailed clear. (Mike told me later that he had indeed lost contact with the mast and had pulled normal red-line max power till I kept shouting, whereupon he pulled "a bit more").

The emergency lift had caused an enormous swing on the 60-70 feet of cable we had out. When Mike brought the aircraft to a very high hover to the side of the ship I pulled and pushed on the wire to damp out the swing.

Our spotlights had been trained on the ship so it was some time before Rick could get our winch spot trained on the survivors who, until the swing reduced, were alternately out to the right or out of sight behind the aircraft. I winched in and as they came into the light we saw that they were women. As they came closer there was a sudden exclamation from Rick, "They've got kids!". Then we saw that the kids were not in the strops but had been put down the clothing and were simply being held by the women. I slowed the winch and gingerly brought them up to the door. Rick and I had agreed to grab one child each, but the women pre-empted us by turning and tumbling the 6 and 3 year-olds onto the floor. We handed the kids over to Hamish Grant then brought the women on board, one momentarily collapsing at our feet.

The time was 1.17am, four rescued, 18 to go, in pairs – 9 more lifts. Then we saw that the Hi-line was hanging below us and was not on the ship. Mike was the first to say it, but we all agreed that the trail was too time consuming and we'd have to find another way of getting the Hi-line onto the ship. First, we had to recover the rope – 300 feet hand over hand with 7kg on the end! While we were doing this, we got the German vessel Walter Herwig to move ahead and provide a hover reference for Mike. Once that was done, we re-surveyed the top bridge and decided that, to winch well clear of the mast, we'd get the remaining crew to move in pairs outside the guard-rail onto the yellow plastic roof over the outer navigation deck. This roof was of similar dimensions to a cricket wicket and I thought that if I threw the weight at the forward end it would drift back onto the middle of the 'wicket'. At the first attempt the weight flew along the 'wicket' and sailed off the back end. I had to talk Mike into a position in space a few yards ahead of the 'wicket' and chuck the weight into the wind. The next attempt was successful and as the weight slid across the roof one of the crew made a great diving stop.

Mike and I agreed a way of hauling the crew off at an angle to minimise the swing and over the next few lifts got quite good at it. Then suddenly the sky lit up. From the rear of the weather deck a massive fireball erupted. We were alarmed at first as it expanded towards us but for a change we were glad of the 70 knots of wind across the deck which squashed the forward progress of the flames and held them away from us. A spectacular globule of flaming gas broke away and rose into the night, extinguishing 200 feet or so above the ship. As quick as it had erupted it died away and we wondered if this was a one-off. We continued the lifts until we had 14 survivors on board and Mike called a break to massage his stiff neck as on every lift he had been craning his neck to see the ship. Dave Simpson, who took over the flying, had had the worst of jobs. He had been briefed by Mike to monitor the instruments and be ready to take over at any time Mike was unable to continue or became disorientated. Dave had been watching the instruments on the blind side of the aircraft and in particular the radar altimeter which was swinging between 40 and 150 feet as towering waves passed in the corner of his eye. This was causing him to feel seasick but he kept his mouth shut. Dave was also working the radios with the ship and the Nimrod and as we sat and observed the ship during our break, he pointed out an outrageous sight. The crew had been asked to remove obstructions and as there was no longer access to tools stored in the stern, the ship's cook was hanging on to a stanchion mounted on the forward bulwark and hacking down a fibreglass aerial with a meat cleaver, seemingly oblivious to the pounding seas on the bow immediately below! Unfortunately cutting down one of the aerials cut off our direct link to the ship and it was only through the Nimrod that we were to re-establish indirect comms.

During the break the Coastguard gave us some information on the hazardous nature of the cargo and after a brief discussion we all thought we should just get on with the job as quickly as possible. There was then another explosive ball of fire, much the same as the last one. On the next but one lift, as helpers were thinning out, a crewman, unseen by us, hitched the Hi-line to the guard-rail while he was helping his mates into the strops. He forgot to undo it and, as we lifted them off, the Hi-line weak link did its job. We were reduced to our last Hi-line but got it aboard without much difficulty, however, the Captain, checking progress and no doubt looking out for his turn, left the wheelhouse where he, by then, had been steering on his own. The ship veered sharply to starboard and, with the next pair pulling in the strops, we had to make a dash to keep up with the turn and soon found ourselves over the seat of the fire on the weather deck. It was like looking down on a giant glowing barbecue and I remember Rick saying "We don't want to be here!". The Captain was only away from the wheel for a few seconds before he dashed back and sorted the problem, enabling us to complete the next lift.

We now had 18 survivors on board with seats for 16. The aircraft was becoming tail-heavy and Mike was having trouble controlling it. We had to get Hamish Grant to act as 'whipper-in' and push people forward.

There was then another fireball which we thought was slightly worse than its predecessors, and after it subsided we lifted the penultimate pair. With no little excitement we returned the strops for the last pair and saw the first mate bang on the wheelhouse roof with a fire axe. The captain, a tall long-legged chap, raced out of the wheelhouse and, with two enormous leaps up the ladder, reached the top bridge. A torch flash and they were on their way. Job done. Time 2.05am.

Rick and I were pumped up with adrenaline and when these two big Swedish seamen arrived at the door we got Mike to control the winch and bodily lifted them across the cabin and plonked them on the seats as if they had been lightweight kids. I had no wish to waste time hauling-in the Hi-line so ditched it, stowed the winch hook, closed the cabin door and gave Mike the clearance to "get the hell out of here!". I took one last look at the unmanned Finneagle, framed in the door window, still powering through the night, then turned to share a 'high-five' with Rick. Dave Simpson gave us a steer for Kirkwall where Mike landed a heavy, wallowing aircraft at 2.30am. As the engines wound down we could hear and feel the 40 knot wind rattling the tail rotor blades but it was lovely to be on solid ground after the gyrations of the past few hours. The odd experiences of the night, however, were not over. Lucky to have a seat in my radar cabin, I watched fascinated as the survivors started moving towards the forward exit door, hands in pockets, looking just like unconcerned commuters getting off the local bus. It was such a contrast with the way they had entered this helicopter just a few minutes beforehand.

Orkney Coastguard had whipped the crew off for a hospital check up in the town by the time we finished the shutdown checks. Hamish had had little to do medical-wise, one crewman suffered a broken arm securing the cargo, two had minor leg injuries and two were suffering from shock. We went into the terminal for a coffee and had a chat with the crew of Rescue 17 before they departed for Sumburgh. We had all felt fit enough to go straight back to Lossiemouth after refuelling but then the airport staff told us a BBC Scotland TV crew were just landing. After half an hour of interviews where we re-lived the night's entertainment we were shattered; the adrenaline had evaporated and we were done. Each of us felt the same. So off to the metropolis of Kirkwall at 4.30 in the morning. The Coastguard drove us to the Royal Hotel at the harbour. It was apparent policy not to take rescuers and survivors to the same accommodation. We saw in later TV broadcasts that the survivors' hotel had opened the bar. The night porter at the Royal very kindly found us a can of beer and a whisky miniature each. We stood and chatted outside his office and listened to the account of our escapades on the 5am news, then to bed at around 5.30.

Rick and I shared a room and after wringing out our sweat-sodden clothing, hung it over the radiator, hoping we might not be disturbed till midday when the kit might be dry. I lay in my bed staring at the ceiling, still wound up, with images and events churning through my mind. A combination of orange street lights, wavy patterns on the curtains and a slight draught created dancing images on the ceiling very reminiscent of the flames on Finneagle. After half an hour of this I couldn't take any more and whispered "You awake?". "Yeah", said Rick. We chatted for ages and knew we wouldn't sleep tonight.

Eventually we decided to get up and find a payphone to warn our families what we'd been up to. The clothing was now cold and wet but at least we could look forward to a decent Scottish breakfast. Eventually when the dining room opened we sat down and ordered everything that was going. I was just waiting for my kippers when Mike came in and said, "Eat up lads, Station Commander wants us back at Lossiemouth for a press conference at 11 o'clock!". No rest for the wicked!

Flight Lieutenant Michael Lakey was awarded the George Medal.

Flight Lieutenant William Campbell was awarded the Air Force Cross.

Sergeant Richard Bragg was awarded the Air Force Medal.

Squadron Leader Doctor Hamish Grant was awarded The Queen's Commendation for Valuable Service In The Air.

Flight Lieutenant David Simpson was awarded The Queen's Commendation for Valuable Service in the Air.

All five of these crew members were awarded the Silver Medal of the Swedish Society for the Rescue of Shipwrecked Seamen.

The crew were the first recipients of the Edward & Maisie Lewis Award from the Shipwrecked Fishermen and Mariners Royal Benevolent Society.

Flight Lieutenant Michael Lakey, Royal Air Force, was awarded the International Helicopter Heroism Award from the Aviation & Spacewriters Guild of the USA.

He was also decorated and embraced by The Order of the Golden Lions of Sweden,

He was voted '1980 Scot of the Year' by Radio Scotland listeners.

Several of the awards were accompanied by generous cheques to the RAF Benevolent Fund.

The Johannson Group, owners of Finneagle, presented the crew with a replica ship's bell with an engraved plaque which reads:

"The crew members, their families and the owners of Finneagle express their gratitude for the most courageous rescue of all on board the vessel when she was burning and in a gale and had to be abandoned at 3.10 on October 2, 1980. The bravery and endurance of the crew are beyond all praise."

Chapter Fourteen

Diver Rescue

Richard Mcleod, Diving Consultant

Saturation diving is an unusual way to earn a living to put it mildly.

It supersedes the original bell diving operations from a 'Support Ship' with a 'moonpool' (an opening in the centre of a marine vessel that permits divers easier and safer access into and exit from the sea) and diving bell deployment system. This consists of a main winch attached to the top of the bell, a double wired winch, and an umbilical winch which supplies breathing mixtures, power, heating water, plus voice and visual communications with the surface. Two, or three divers enter the underside of the bell via a vertical two ft long 'trunk'. This has a metal door at either end – one opening inwards – and the other outwards. After climbing into the bell, the bottom door is shut and the bell winched down guide wires, which stop it from spinning and can be used as an emergency recovery device. Water pressure builds up as the depth increases holding the lower door clamped shut. On arrival at 'working depth' which in the North Sea can be anything from 20 to 140 meters, the internal bell pressure is still at one atmosphere. The vessel moves into the most appropriate position and the 'working diver' prepares his equipment for 'locking out'. The 'bell man' communicates with the Diving supervisor in the topside control centre and when all are ready the 'Dive Time' Commences as the bell is pressurised via the bell umbilical and various control valves, until it reaches the same pressure as the seawater outside. The bottom door can now be opened without water entering the bell but allowing the diver access to the worksite via the trunk. The 'Bell Man' pays out the divers' umbilical which carries- like the bell umbilical- a supply of breathing gas, hot water, and communications, to the diver, as well as being a life line. So far so good, and all being well, the diver can carry out the predetermined tasks.

However, there are other factors to consider such as the effect of the pressure on the body. At 100 meters this is 10 times the atmospheric pressure that our bodies are used to. Descending is no problem- it can be done in less than 5 minutes, but below 50 meters nitrogen in the air becomes toxic, and 5 times the normal quantity of oxygen begins to play havoc with our respiratory systems. This is countered by using helium (an inert gas) and a much lower percentage of oxygen such as 90% helium and 4% oxygen. The diver's depth and 'pressured up' time is closely monitored by the Supervisor above in the installation.

The big problem is decompression on recovery of the diver to the surface, where the pressure remains, of course, at one atmosphere. The duration of decompression has to be carefully calculated in order to avoid getting the "Bends". Oxygen is no problem as the body uses this up, but the inert gas, whether nitrogen or helium, has to circulate round the blood stream and be exhaled from the lungs. Too rapid a decompression can cause these gasses to form increasing sized bubbles which can get stuck- particularly in joint areas. Even mild incidence of the bends is painful. The remedy is to increase the Bell pressure until the pain goes and then continue decompression more slowly allowing the inert gas to be expelled via the lungs. In the old days, working at 120 meters, it could take as long as 15 hours to decompress back to atmospheric pressure after a 1 hour bell dive.

As the offshore Oil Business expanded in the 1970s, subsea work became essential. Structures, pipelines and wellheads had to be installed and maintained, requiring ever more diving hours. Larger de-compression chambers were incorporated on the decks of the dive support ships. The Dive Systems were improved so that the Bell could be lowered and clamped onto the chamber. Once the pressure inside the bell and the chamber was equalized, the inner door of the bell 'trunk' and the upper door of the chamber could be opened allowing the divers to pass through. Room to get out of cumbersome diving gear and into a hot shower, followed by a long sleep whilst decompression was completed. Meals could be passed in via a double doored horizontal trunk in the side of the chamber. Simple principal – the divers shut and seal the inside door, the pressure is evacuated by the external dive technician who then loads the food or equipment and clamps the outer door shut. A valve then allows the pressure from inside the chamber to equalize the trunk so that the inner door can be opened. Sounds complicated, but in reality doesn't take very long.

Saturation diving and multi-inter-connected chambers evolved from these relatively simple beginnings.

Firstly – rather than decompressing divers after each dive, a team of usually 6 divers enter a chamber at ambient (deck) pressure via a short horizontal sealable trunk. A chamber usually has 6 bunk beds with an offshoot living/eating area and a toilet & shower compartment. There will be a vertical sealable trunk leading up to a hatch way onto which the bell-bottom entry can be clamped as required. Usually there will be 2 or 3 other similar inter-connecting chambers plus an emergency recovery lock on facility. Using air locks these can all be maintained at different pressures if the work sites are at different depths. Additionally there can often be 2 separate diving bells, which can lock onto different trunks if required.

A routine would start by one of the 3 two-man man teams being 'called to arms' by the dive Supervisor- It might take an hour to dress, prepare and get a full briefing of the job in hand, before climbing up into the bell to start the dive. The Chamber and Bell are both pressurised already to the required working depth.

A typical deep dive will last for six hours – split half and half between the two divers, as one man is always monitoring the bell, tending the diver's umbilical, and could act as a rescuer should an emergency arise. At the end of this the bell is recovered and locked back onto the Chamber. An hour is allocated for a shower, change of gear, meal and a full de-briefing. This scenario could be repeated round the clock using the other two teams.

If required, three pairs of divers will stay under pressure for up to two weeks. At the end of this they will be slowly depressurized in their chamber which might take up to five days.

At the same time, other chambers (sometimes two or more) can still be used by other teams of divers. A separate chamber control room is manned 100% of the time by about six 'Dive Techs'. Their duty is to monitor and control the depth, pressures, gas mixtures, heat, lighting, video and voice communications and provide food and comfort as needed. There will also be a deck crew who work the deployment winches and lock the bell on and off the 'trunking. There will frequently be requirements for ancillary equipment and tools

Fortunately, accidents and emergencies were infrequent, but if they happened, they could be very serious, and they had to be prepared for. Choppers were our difference between life and death. A worst-case scenario would be if a diver was injured whilst on the job. His partner would have to lock out, assess the problem and get him back into the bell- followed by himself and the 2 x 30 meter diver umbilicals – not an easy task. Obviously, the Supervisor in the Dive controller would be fully involved. At this stage, if necessary, he could brief the Ship's medical officer and prepare to lock in a trained medic and emergency equipment into the topside decompression chamber.

Once the injured diver is securely in the bell he can be recovered to the surface and locked onto the chamber. This might take about 30 to 45 minutes – but would also depend in the state of the diver.

Once again, depending on the urgency of the diver's condition, the ship's Captain could summon assistance from the shoreside emergency facilities, which would be able to send out a helicopter and an experienced hyperbaric doctor. What one can never do, however, is rapidly decompress the injured diver. There are facilities on board to lock a single man into a 'decompression capsule' onto the entry lock of the living chamber of the dive complex. Once maneuvered and locked on the emergency chamber internal pressure can be equalized with the living chamber and the patient transferred through.

It is then a matter of closing the airtight doors, disconnecting the emergency chamber and transporting it up to the helideck. No mean task as it could easily weigh over 500kg.

From Peter Saxton –

A helicopter would be summoned either from in-field if one is available and suitable, but from an onshore base if not. The aircraft would take full fuel prior to take-off and if it was typically a S61 would have a cabin attendant as well as the two pilots and a doctor. It would be allocated a priority call-sign prefixed with the word "Medivac" (Medical Evacuation). This callsign takes precedence over all others except a "Mayday" emergency. The pilots could be confident that the Air Traffic Controllers would direct other traffic out of their flight path. On landing at the installation, the rescue helicopter would be shut down, both rotors and engines.

From Richard McLeod –

So the patient has now been transferred into a capsule installed within the DS. This capsule would then be moved from the DS up to the helideck sealed to transport the diver to hospital still under pressure to protect him from the Bends. The capsule is lifted onto the helicopter and secured within the cabin under supervision of the cabin attendant.

Peter Saxton –

The engines are started, the rotors engaged, the aircraft cleared for take-off. The Captain was briefed that the return to the mainland should be flown at low-level and in any case not above 1000 feet above sea-level to guard against the eventuality that the protecting capsule might have a fault. Air pressure at low level is higher than at altitude and therefore any tendency to decompress would be minimised.

On one occasion when I was involved in such an operation with an AS332 Super Puma the visibility just about qualified for visual flight rules, but wasn't great, so Air Traffic said I could use the Instrument Landing System (ILS) to runway 17 at Aberdeen Dyce Airport, then fly down the runway over Aberdeen City turning to land into wind on the helipad at Forester Hill Hospital. We did not reduce to instrument approach speed but kept the speed up to minimise the time to landing and it worked a treat although it must have rattled a few windows. We touched down on the helipad and shut the aircraft down. The capsule was off-loaded, I think by a fork-lift truck, and trundled up the connecting path towards a marvellous facility called the Hyperbaric Unit, which is still operating today.

Richard McLeod –

The capsule with the diver in it would then be moved through an airlock into a compression complex. The airlocks would be closed. The compression complex was pressurised to the same pressure as the diver had been experiencing on the bed of the North Sea. The capsule would then be opened, and the diver extracted. A medical team was ready to receive him, examine, prepare, and carry out the necessary procedure. The team, within the sealed operating facility, was at the same atmospheric pressure as the diver. During the recovery and decompression, which might take days, the medical team remained inside the Hyperbaric complex to attend the patient and of course to allow them also to decompress at a safe rate.

Peter Saxton –

In the intervening years since I ceased professional flying I have often recalled these operations with a sense of admiration. They demanded close cooperation between many professional units including divers, engineers, installation ops staff, helicopter ops and technical staff, helicopter crew and air traffic control units. However, without wishing to diminish anyone else's efforts, the technical staff who operated the Aberdeen Royal Infirmary Hyperbaric Unit and the life-saving medical teams who staffed the operating theatre in such an extraordinary environment were truly special.

Chapter Fifteen

Ditchings – The Ditchings of G-BEID

Captain David Paul

On 31st January 1980, I arrived at the Flight Briefing room at Dyce Airport, before Captain Ian Recton, to start planning our flight that morning. Although I was below him on the almighty seniority list we decided that I would sign as Commander for our first flight, and he as Commander for our second.

The first was a simple enough trip – out to the British Gas contracted semi-submersible driller 'Atlantic II' and back. To give British Gas the maximum flexibility we would route out via a refuel on the 'Auk' production platform at 150 miles, as the 'Atlantic II' was positioned 180 miles from Aberdeen and the lower fuel figure outbound would give them the higher payload they wanted. The outbound legs were uneventful and once on the deck of the 'Atlantic II' we picked up our 13 inbound passengers and then climbed to Flight Level 45 for the return leg direct to Aberdeen. This gave us a chance of good VHF contact with 'Highland Radar' in the days before extra offshore relay stations. The slack winds that day meant that the leg should have taken about 1hr and 40 minutes. Ian and I eventually ran out of intelligent topics of conversation, such as whether the Navy or the Air Force was best, and objects for 'I Spy' and then just watched the sea and clouds passing slowly by outside.

Every few minutes I scanned the temperatures and pressures in the double row of gauges down the centre of the instrument panel. With a feeling of foreboding I noticed a slight rise in the main gearbox oil temperature when we were about halfway between the 'Auk' and Aberdeen. After pointing it out to Ian we made a careful note of the exact reading and time and determined to check it again in a couple of minutes. However, our eyes were inexorably drawn to that gauge and it very soon became clear that the temperature was rising and also that the pressure was slowly falling – the required 'double indication'- and all the proof we needed that there was a real problem. At that time there were no helidecks on that radial inside the 'Auk' so onward we flew.

Speaking to our passengers later, in the life-raft, several of them stated that they had heard a muffled bang above the cabin, shortly followed by another similar sound. It turned out that the first noise was caused by one of the matched pair of belts which drive the transmission oil cooler fan snapping and hitting the small deck area underneath and the second was when it snagged the remaining belt and broke that off as well. We were then left with no main gearbox oil cooling.

We briefed the passengers that there was a problem with the aircraft but that it did not appear to need any immediate actions on their part apart from checking their immersion suits were securely done up. Likewise, Highland Radar were informed with a Pan call and a Mk 2 Shackleton that was airborne and monitoring the Highland Radar frequency decided he would come and fly around closer to our bit of the sky, which was nice. There was a Sea King airborne from RAF Lossiemouth on a mission quite a way up to the north, but more of that later.

Those that needed to be 'in the know' were all now 'in the know' so we consulted the Emergency Checklist to make sure we did everything in the right order and on cue. The Checklist was quite unequivocal – when the main gearbox oil temperature reached 150 degrees centigrade (with the double indication of falling pressure) we were to 'land immediately'. As the sea was calm there was no point in trying to heroically stagger as far as Girdle Ness or some suitable landing spot ashore and risking some catastrophic gearbox failure. We had 13 passengers to look after on a calm day and that was that.

The Elinor Viking – Lerwick 1977.

BAH Chinook arrives Dyce airport, June 1981.

Bond AS332L Super Puma landing on offshore platform 1983.

British Airways Helicopters BV234LR Chinook circles The Magnus Platform 1986.

BAH Chinook in the Magnus Field with Polycastle semi-submersible rig 1986.

BAH Chinook, Bullers Of Buchan, Aberdeenshire.

Grandpa – the first S61 delivered to British European Airways.

BAH Chinook landing Treasure Finder semi-submersible rig.

Reflections from the helideck.

Cockpit of a BAH S61-radar screen on central consol, moving map at top.

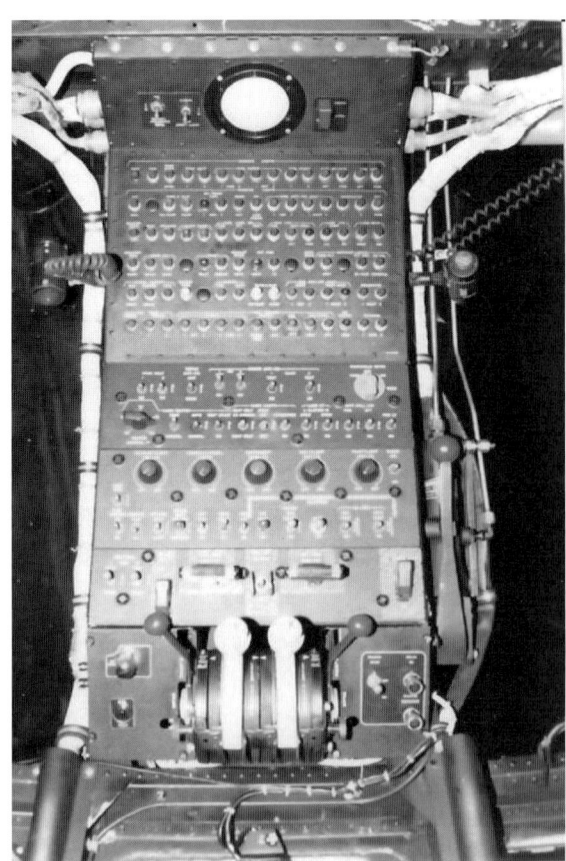

Overhead panel Sikorsky S61N.

Chinook landing on Fulmar platform.

Early morning low level arrival from an S61.

Offshore refuelling.

Winching rescue.

Piper Alpha ablaze – British International Helicopters S61.

Piper Alpha with MV Tharos in attendance.

S61 take off from an offshore heliceck. Undercarriage partially retracted.

S61 en route on a calm day.

Penrod sea state 3/4. A ditched helicopter would probably capsize.

S61 shut down on the Penrod.

Sumburgh line up.

S61 underslinging a heavy load.

S61 water landing.

A British International Helicopters Super Puma.

RAF Wessex.

British International Helicopters BV234LR Chinook.

S61 deck landing on Treasure Finder in a storm.

Treasure Finder – 8-legged semi submersible drilling rig against a production platform in a storm.

We crept slowly closer to the coast but the inevitable 150 degrees moment arrived at about 20 miles off the coast and we prepared to ditch – Ian had the exciting task of transmitting a real 'Mayday' call. I landed facing into what we thought the surface wind was, although it was really only a very light breeze. We still had a working machine, albeit with a hot gearbox, and decided that we might water taxi it towards Aberdeen. If there were any further problems, we could just shut it down and jump in the life-rafts. The problem with this plan soon became apparent as there was a large swell from the north and the aircraft rolled quite alarmingly from time to time, up to about 15 degrees. If we had accidentally discovered the capsize angle of an S61N (without sponson flotation bags in those days) when burning and turning, we would have made things unnecessarily difficult for ourselves.

After shutting down Ian managed to deploy the sea anchor from its awkwardly positioned box (after removing his window), while I monitored whichever radio used the upper aerial and told the Shackleton, now on-scene SAR commander, what was going on. He told us that the RAF Sea King would not be with us for some time as it still had to complete another rescue task. I learned later that it was being flown by Flt Lt Mike Lakey, a chum I used to sit next to at school, and that another schoolmate, Robbie Sutton, was frequently his winchman. It was nearly an interesting reunion of old boys from the City of Bath Technical School and he later told me he was about 5 minutes away when the rescue of our passengers was completed. Three months later Mike went on to distinguish himself by an amazing night rescue from the Swedish freighter Finneagle, adrift and on fire off Orkney. He lifted 22 men, women and children off the ship that night in appalling conditions. He was justifiably awarded the George Medal. He had been in London that very morning to attend a press conference regarding his crew's part in the Alexander Kielland rescue – 123 people died when a leg broke off a semi-submersible drilling rig (converted for accommodation).

It was now time to test the life-raft out and so Ian walked back through the aircraft and after removing the rear escape door he pushed the life-raft out and eventually, after reaching the end of the lanyard, pulled hard and the raft inflated. Wishing to secure the raft while the passengers jumped into it, he discovered that the requisite cleat had been removed by a 'secret' modification, so the line had to be secured to something else. The passengers duly disembarked into the raft and after switching everything off in the cockpit I followed hot on their heels. It was calm, sunny and quiet, apart from the drone of the Shackleton orbiting overhead and we started discussing the situation with the passengers.

They were all in good spirits, apart from one who wanted his attaché case out of the aircraft and moaned about missing his flight to London. It broke the ice and Ian busied himself with taking the sea sickness tablets from the life-raft's first aid kit. The instructions were to 'take with water' but he managed to get them down without as he felt his need to be very urgent. Cue a cruel joke about RAF 'crabs', but even Horatio Nelson was seasick!

Sometime later, after flashing up the SARBE from the life-raft and keeping the Shackleton up to date we were informed that one of our company aircraft was on its way to winch us all. That was good news but the standard S61N did not have any height hold or autopilot facilities so had to be hovered manually. We were sitting in a calm sea with no horizon and no hover references, so they were difficult conditions even for a well drilled crew and our SAR crews did not practise very often, which soon became apparent. The sound of an approaching helicopter was followed by the sight of a company S61N (G-BEDI) approaching through the mist. When a hover had finally been established, one of the Company crewmen, George Edge, descended on the winch wire and eventually found his way to the dinghy. Using a double harness, he put one of the passengers into the sling and gave the thumbs up to the man in the helicopter doorway.

The two of them went out of the life-raft like a cork from a bottle, pitching Ian into the sea, and eventually reaching the cabin door.

After thirty minutes more winching a North Sea supply boat arrived and offered us the welcome news that the Aberdeen Lifeboat would shortly be arriving. We sat in the life-raft during that time, alongside the supply boat with its scrambling nets rigged. It would be easier to transfer to the lifeboat from the life-raft than from the supply boat and although the supply boat was outbound to a rig it would of course delay its passage until further help arrived. George had arrived from the helicopter again and remained to assist as required.

With the lifeboat alongside us the supply boat continued on its way and the crew and remaining passengers were helped on board. George went swimming and attached a line to the sea anchor attachment under the aircraft's nose and after paying out a suitable length of towrope we started off towards Aberdeen Harbour. Salvage attempts with ditched S61s and Sea Kings in the past had tried to tow by attaching to the tail wheel, which invariably pulled the tail wheel assembly from the fuselage, usually sinking the aircraft. A Bristow S61N now appeared and proceeded to winch up the remaining passengers, followed by Ian and me. I was delighted to come face to face with their crewman, the late Colin Larcombe in the aircraft doorway, not having seen him since 819 Naval Air Squadron at Prestwick some five years before.

Ian and I were examined medically and declared fit on return. The Company fielded the attentions of the Press. The helicopter was towed into Aberdeen Harbour and lifted onto a jetty where it was sprayed with large amounts of fresh water. The main rotor blades were removed, and a tractor towed it back to Dyce where it was put in a restricted access hangar to await inspection by the AAIB and our engineers. Ian and I gave our accounts of the event to an inspector from the AAIB, a nominated British Airways mainline investigator and our own Captain Tony Buckley over the next few days. G-BEID was minutely inspected for any damage or corrosion and returned to service a week or two later.

The cause of the loss of cooling was confirmed as the breakage of one of the fan belts which then fouled the other. A batch of fan belts had come into contact with acid during manufacture and when Sikorsky found out they had advised all their customers, but our engineers had assumed that the advice referred to non-Sikorsky supplied spares and took no action. Sod's Law ensured that our aircraft had the only belts from that batch in the BAH fleet. Sikorsky had also advised all S61 operators that if transmission oil cooling was lost, as in our case, then the gearbox temperature would rise to between 180 to 210 degrees centigrade and that it would lubricate everything adequately enough for the aircraft to reach its destination. The problem was that the temperature gauges fitted at the time only read up to 180c so we would have had no way of knowing when the temperature had stabilised. New gauges were fitted as soon as possible and the emergency checklist eventually amended.

They say that lightning doesn't strike in the same place twice, but it did for Ian Recton. Ian ditched again, in G-ASNL, another S61, with Captain Tony Buckley, near Occidental's Claymore platform in March 1983. The ditching was more dramatic the second time and he took up an offer of a position back in the Royal Air Force, saying at the time that he thought it the safer option from a flying and maintenance point of view.

The Last Flight of G-BEID

G-BEID continued in service with British Airways Helicopters and then with British International Helicopters, which was the new name of the company after British Airways decided that helicopters were not part of its 'core business' and sold it to Robert Maxwell.

On the 13th July 1988 Captain Ian Sutherland was in command of Sikorsky S61 G-BEID into Sumburgh from the East Shetland Basin when a fire started in the vicinity of one of its engines. He ditched the aircraft successfully with a double fire indication 29 miles north east of Sumburgh in the Shetland Islands. After the 19 passengers and 2 crew had abandoned the aircraft and taken to the life rafts, most of the fuselage was consumed by fire and the wreckage eventually sank.

The cause of the fire was a failure of the number 5 bearing in number 2 engine.

The story is taken up by his Co-pilot for the day, Captain Malcolm McDougall.

We had departed from the Safe Felicia, attached to the Eider Platform, taking a work team who had been engaged on the establishment of this new Shell platform. I was the Handling Pilot on what was our second trip that day.

As we reached 35 miles to go to land at Sumburgh, we had talked for a while and now returned to a companionable silence, each concentrating on our appointed tasks. I had a strange sensation of having felt, or heard something, but was unsure as to exactly what it was.

It emerged later, when Ian and I attended the technical debrief at Royal Aircraft Establishment Farnborough, that I had sensed the engine malfunction. The No. 5. bearing had disintegrated, causing severe friction in the area and with the bearing gone, oil being pumped out under pressure over very hot metal. This blow-torch effect was playing back on the magnesium alloy gearbox, which then ignited into a searingly hot magnesium-fire.

In the cabin, an engineer in row three, more or less underneath the gearbox, heard a sharp cracking sound. In the cockpit, though, our first positive sign was a No. 2. engine fire-warning light. We discussed the unusual engine indications, in that both engines were matched and normal. Therefore, it was a further 20 seconds, after I had looked over my right shoulder and reported that there was white smoke swirling down from the cabin roof, that we responded to the electrical indication of engine-fire and completed the shut-down drills on the No. 2. Engine.

Perhaps 30 seconds later I called

"Fire-Warning No. 1."

I, as the handling pilot, was turning right towards the land and descending, as we were only about 12 miles east of the Out Skerries Islands. Further discussion produced the agreement that we would not shut down this engine, as while it was running it would allow us to make a controlled ditching. There were no corroborating indications from the engine-instruments.

During this second minute of the emergency, we surely both thought we were doomed. The manifestations of our problems were quite unlike any drills we had simulated in training. Time seemed to drag; there was an acrid smell of burning wafting forward from the cabin. It was a smell that stayed with me for many years".

"We were quite heavy and the remaining engine was up to its limit. Ian took control at this point and I was then free to open the port cockpit window and put my head out, holding onto my headphones to prevent them being pulled off by the slipstream. The strange thing is that I have no memory of what I saw. Only later, at Royal Aircraft Establishment (RAE) Farnborough, did I hear my own voice from the Cockpit Voice Recorder reporting,

"We are seriously on fire."

This is called Stress-Related Memory-Loss. I was so appalled at the sight of smoke and flames billowing back in a trail behind the aircraft, that my mind immediately irradicated this vision from my memory.

We began to prepare for the ditching, with a Mayday call, a passenger brief and a completion of the checks. Ian then ordered me to inflate the sponson floats, which I did.

We were below 100 feet flying at 67 knots as Ian brought up the nose for the final commitment to the sea. We ditched into the sea and as we hit the waves I saw the sea green on the forward windscreen. The aircraft settled back nicely to a stable rolling, bobbing motion. This whole sequence of events took only 3 minutes, 8 seconds! We later learned that the hydraulic lines had burnt through as Ian found the Rotor-Brake ineffective some thirty seconds later. It is a chilling inference that Main-Rotor control would have been lost after a further short interval. Anyway, this three minutes seemed like a lifetime.

Besides all the actions described, we had experienced a variety of personal thoughts on the dire nature of our emergency and the inference that, with the progressive worsening of the situation, that we may lose control altogether and perish. It has frequently been said in such a situation one has no time to worry, but our thoughts were racing in seconds that dragged like hours. With the helicopter intact in the water, I began to feel more optimistic.

Ian ordered me to jettison the rear port door, though he had to direct my finger to the switch, a further psychological block discussed later with AIB. Apparently, items that are "touched" regularly remain within immediate memory, whereas others are discarded under stress.

The passengers were sitting at the edges of their seats, looking very tense and I was concerned that they may panic and run around impeding my disembarkation drills. I told them to remain seated while I organised the dinghy, then un-clipped the dinghy and dragged it to the door. Because the Life raft had been installed up-side-down, I had the long lanyard in my hand and once outside the cargo door inflated the raft. The thin nylon cord skinned some flesh of my hand as I tried to hold it close to the door.

Happily for us, these 19 passengers were a single company team and were all known to each other, mostly seasoned helicopter travellers and behaved like a disciplined ship's crew. On my call, they filed into the forward dinghy. Beyond Row 3, there was a wall of smoke and I tried to run through it to see how the passengers at the rear were coping. I got only six feet and staggered back, choking. Ian joined me in the cabin at this point and said he would have a go. He was back, spluttering and shaking his head, as quickly as I had been.

Ian joined the passengers in the dinghy and I paused to lean back out of the door, looking up at the engine area, intrigued that the fire had now subsided to a very large degree, although later, it resumed in earnest.

Ian motioned me to join them in the life raft and we cast off, found the paddles and one of the guys, now in his element organised a paddling team. We were happy to let them get on with it.

We exerted considerable effort to get the dinghy moving but after perhaps ten minutes, we paused a hundred or so metres from the scene and watched in awe as the hull was gradually engulfed in a raging fire, the gearbox falling off. Then the fuel tanks exploded in three quite distinct events into a white ball of flame, the great rotor-blades melting and crumbling like wax, until only the Tail-Section was left recognisable.

Twenty minutes later, once again seeming like all afternoon, Bristows Coastguard helicopter arrived. The winching began, the Winchman organising the majority of us into the second dinghy while he took guys up two at a time. The exercise took an hour and was a chilly process, the rotor down-draught lashing us with cold, stinging spray.

I was the last rescué up and I will never forget the final scene being hoisted up, helpless, on the end of a steel wire, being grabbed from death into the safety and warmth of a hovering rescue Sikorsky S61.

I looked out of the port-hole at India Delta as she burned, her tail reaching up at an ungainly angle, stark against the grey skies, a dark skein of smoke trailing away as she sank.

Post Script

Ian and I have had our moments of emotional trauma since then. There have been sleepless nights. The bad dreams stopped after a couple of years. Sometimes they come back.

Chapter Sixteen

Balpa and the Campaign for Flight Safety

Captain Peter Saxton

I arrived on the North Sea in 1977 after ten years' service with the RAF. I had two small children who had to be snuggled up with care in bedrooms in our new house in Balmedie, a village north of Aberdeen, and in that season, I first began to understand the expression 'The hardy Scot.'

It was so cold that ice froze on the inside of my children's bedroom windows. We had nothing approaching central heating. We had a single open Baxi fire which warmed inadequately the ground floor of our house and the hot water. The bedrooms were not heated at all. The open fire would go out during the night if you let it, and I found that one of my new duties was getting up at around 3am to bank up the fire again to keep it alight. Come spring I extended my mortgage and installed central heating – I didn't want to risk another winter like that.

That was the way it was in Aberdeen in that first winter. Poor sheep froze to death in the fields behind us. The police knocked on our doors asking us if we could give stranded people a bed for the night as the snow had drifted high on the roads. The Aberdeen to Inverness railway train got lost in a snowdrift and helicopters had to search for it and direct rescuers to its location.

Helicopter pilots at Dyce Airport, the base at Aberdeen that supported the central sector of the North Sea oil fields, were attracting the attention of the press. Roughly half of the pilots working for Bristow Helicopters were on strike. Bristow Helicopters, the largest of four companies competing for business, was holding a sizeable number of overseas contracts. Pilots employed by Bristow had a basic contract enabling the company to deploy them to man these operations. Many of the pilots had enjoyed overseas postings during their time as military pilots, and one of the attractions of seeking employment with this company was that one could expect overseas postings; ironic then that the ostensible cause of this dispute was the circumstances in which a pilot could be posted overseas. A posting notice would indicate to where the pilots would be posted, and for how long. The dispute was over whether the company was entitled unilaterally to terminate the current posting notice before its stated term, replacing it with another. The company believed it had, and took this action with one particular pilot. The disputing pilots believed it did not, and after a number of increasingly acrimonious meetings, called a strike.

The situation was politically complicated. The pilots claimed that the company was victimizing the pilot in question because they suspected him of recruiting membership for the British Airline Pilots' Association (BALPA), the pilots' union. Bristows management were uncomfortable with the increasing membership of BALPA among their pilots. They feared a strong union membership would limit their ability to manage as they wished. Membership of the union had been rising quickly.

After several weeks of picketing, during which BALPA supported the striking pilots financially, Mark Young, the General Secretary of BALPA delivered a masterstroke. He persuaded a substantial number of the striking Bristow pilots to join British Airways Helicopters, (BAH) the main rival to Bristow for North Sea business. The strategic benefit to BAH was considerable. They were short of crews to the extent that they had not been able to expand their business as they wished, even in a booming North Sea. This move solved that problem practically overnight, and it was directly at the expense of their most serious rival.

Alan Bristow, the ebullient boss of Bristow Helicopters, needed to end the stand-off. It involved accepting that this serious industrial incident would be subjected to a full public enquiry presided over by Lord MacDonald. This was held in Glasgow. Alan Bristow in particular came in for criticism over his style, which the Judge described as more appropriate to the barrack-room than the board-room.

BALPA considered it had probably won on points. However, the incident had cost BALPA a lot of funds, as well as some adverse publicity in the press. Probably the only true winner was British Airways Helicopters, which had gained, free of charge, a substantial number of trained experienced helicopter pilots, and was now in a position to tender credibly for any work going. By late summer 1977, everyone was back at work, albeit many for a new operator.

One legacy of the strike was an atmospheric sharpening of rivalry. There was bad feeling between the pilots who had struck, and those who had refused to do so, which lasted for years. Friendships cooled across the corporate divide, and occasionally ended, sometimes after a bout of bar room acrimony in the Skean Dhu Hotel at Dyce. The sense of being North Sea helicopter crew, which had transcended company boundaries, was substantially diminished. However, North Sea oil and gas exploitation continued to surge upward, and there was a lot of flying to do.

There were some more lasting echoes. BALPA had established a lasting presence on the North Sea, almost exclusively concentrated in one company. In Bristows, union activity faded, or went to ground, for over a decade. The pilots of BAH benefited from active representation with that company on matters to do with flight safety, pay rates and employment conditions. They had the ability, as a group, to take an alternative view to the managers in the company.

Flight Safety

It has been called 'the toughest commute on earth'. Oil companies used to refer to it as 'high speed transport', by which they meant us. Low speed transport would have been ships. To get to an offshore oil installation in a ship would have meant hours cooped up in a rolling vessel, a hazardous transfer on to the installation, and possibly reporting for duty sea-sick as a dog.

Choppers took between 45 and 90 minutes for most rigs. You arrived in reasonable shape, able to go straight on duty. Outbound, the Roustabouts smelled of beer because most of the rigs were dry of alcohol. Inbound, the Roustabouts smelled of shampoo and after-shave – they were on their way home, with other things in mind.

For the crews who flew them, there was a tension between organized pilots, and what might be described as 'the establishment' within the industry, especially over flight safety on the North Sea. This 'establishment' comprised company managers, the Civil Aviation Authority, and the industry representative organization – the British Helicopter Advisory Board (BHAB) – plus the oil companies. The BALPA pilot representatives tended to take a conservative view when it came to issues concerning flight safety risks. The 'establishment' were distinctly more 'light touch' – gung-ho some said.

There were some things 'The Establishment' got right. Aircraft performance and airworthiness regulation were generally of a good standard, as were range and endurance fuel requirements. Research and protection against icing was adequate, and the aircraft were fitted with radar, able to pinpoint rigs from big distances. Importantly, these radars gave information about the disposition of bad weather and lines of thunderstorms.

In the early days, the area navigation system was Decca, and this had to be used with care. Decca was an old system, designed originally to enable amphibious landing craft to hit beaches accurately during the D-Day landings. It was unreliable in conditions such as dawn, dusk, coastlines and certainly anywhere near snow. However, area navigation equipment slowly improved with the introduction of more modern aircraft.

Other problems were not well-handled. One winter, a series of unusually low barometric depressions moved over the North Sea, sometimes referred to as 'Polar lows'. Some aircraft had not been equipped with altimeters that could cope with such extremes, and in these conditions would over-read i.e. indicate to the crew that the height of the aircraft was higher than it actually was. Not only would pilots be given false information about their height above the surface, obviously hazardous, but also the separation system in force relied on aircraft being able to fly an accurate altitude to separate them from opposing traffic. To the incredulity of crews, initially the Civil Aviation Authority (CAA) permitted these aircraft to continue to operate -provided a sticker was attached to the altimeters stating that they were inaccurate! It was imperative that aircraft were equipped with altimeters that could give accurate indications in extreme low-pressure conditions, where, of course, it was most needed.

BALPA threatened to make a public fuss about it, and I believe this must have been instrumental in persuading the CAA to withdraw the permission. Looking back, we suspected this had been a classic example of 'regulatory capture', although we called it something very much ruder at the time.

Another argument included the wisdom of allowing fuel jettison to be taken into account in performance calculations, with the CAA allowing it, and BALPA arguing that blowing large quantities of vaporizing fuel out of an aircraft in emergencies that might involve a fire, was not an intelligent idea.

The standard passenger weight was calculated at 187lb for load and balance purposes. Eventually, after empirical research showed this to be a significant underestimation, it was changed to a more realistic figure. However, this took years, and it was sobering to think that during the period prior to the change, aircraft had regularly been flying over the North Sea over-loaded.

One *cause célèbre* concerned the issue of whether helicopters should carry cabin attendants. This was summarized by an 'Insight' feature in *The Sunday Times* in 1976. A North Sea equipped Sikorsky S61 helicopter could accommodate 19 passengers. The aircraft was an amphibian – it could take off and alight on both land and water, and this was considered an important safety consideration for an aircraft destined to spend so much of its time flying over the North Sea. The trouble was that its ability to land on the sea was only cleared for waves up to Sea-State 3, and most of the time the North Sea was much rougher than that. In such circumstances it was likely that once the rotor had been stopped, the aircraft, with its high centre of gravity, would turn upside down and sink. The cabin had only two exits, and all these things contributed to the nightmare scenario that in an evacuation unsupervised by a cabin attendant, disoriented and panicking passengers would be unable to exit the aircraft efficiently, and would drown. This risk was obviously much increased at night, and in the northern regions, the night is long, and dark, and cold. Many pilots believed it was essential therefore, that the minimum crew of a S61 should be three, and should include a cabin attendant. The 'establishment' did not accept this argument, presumably on the grounds that an extra crew member would incur more costs and degrade payload capacity.

Their partial answer, after some years, was 'The Dunker'. This comprised a helicopter cockpit and cabin mock-up, suspended on a powered gantry over a large tank filled with cold water to about twenty feet depth. It was a machine similar to ones that had been used for some time for crew emergency training by the military. The 'fuselage' was dropped onto the water from about five to ten feet, then immediately submerged and turned upside down by the powered gantry. When all the vibration stopped, (simulating the point that the rotor had stopped turning) everyone inside had to evacuate through the emergency exits. From inside the contraption the view was dark and restricted, with cold water rushing in and rising rapidly as the cabin inverted and sank. The occupants had to wait until the water was just about to rise over their heads, take a last deep gulp of air, and remain strapped in their seats holding their breath until the vibrations ceased. Then, in the event, up to nineteen of them had to release their seat belts, swim their way underwater to an exit, and evacuate from the inverted fuselage in an orderly fashion ('non-competitively' to use the CAA's expression). If they were lucky enough to actually get out they then had to identify which way the surface was, and swim up towards it. Disorientation was usual, and to say that all this was a tall order would be an obvious understatement, especially at night. The Dunker could produce wave action to make things even more interesting. In the Dunker though, divers protected us. They waited underwater, ready to grab and pull out anyone who looked as though they were not going to make it. In the North Sea, we would have no such luxury. The training in my time was voluntary for passengers, presumably because it was daunting, but mandatory for crew. Yet cabin attendants themselves were never made mandatory for aircraft equipped to carry not more than 19 passengers. The 'establishment' view prevailed.

However, the establishment mantra that 'our record is good' sounded ignorantly complacent to many of those of us actually doing the flying and who had a voice to say so. That did not include all helicopter pilots by any means. It depended on which company you worked for. Questions surrounding overall safety remained and it seemed clear that the role and attitude of the regulator – the CAA – was key. Only a regulatory body could talk to the oil companies on anything like equal terms, but the CAA appeared to us to be reluctant to use the power bestowed on it. We felt let down. Fatal accidents continued to occur, such as the crash in 1983 of a BAH S61 into the sea between Penzance and the Scilly Isles in very poor visibility. Twenty of the twenty-six passengers died. This disaster is especially harrowing to me as I was asked to attend the Coroner's Court as technical advisor to Queens' Council engaged by BALPA to represent the pilots. The Coroner returned a non-culpable verdict.

"Up to half a million helicopter flights take place off-shore each year…. As yet, (1993) the CAA was said to have failed as an effective regulator and appeared to lack familiarity with the rigours of helicopter travel in the offshore environment." (*Paying For The Piper*, Woolfson, Foster and Beck, P423).

A review of helicopter safety was promised in 1993 after three major disasters *viz* the BIH Chinook Foxtrot Charlie, the BIH S61 Brent

Spa crash, and the Bristow Super Puma Cormorant Alpha disaster, three accidents in six years resulting in sixty-two helicopter fatalities. I had left North Sea flying in 1990, so this was after my time.

Woolfson, Foster and Beck in their excellent work *Paying For The Piper* reported thus: "Overall, since 1969 a total of 113 men had died as a result of helicopter accidents in the UK sector of the North Sea..." (Ibid P424).

The statistics relating to non-fatal reportable accidents also tell a story – the story of the close calls that were averted, just about, including ditching in conditions which, mercifully, allowed rescue of the occupants; or of stricken aircraft that made it back by the skin of their teeth.

Deeply dissatisfied, BALPA had decided to try other, more political channels. It had its own monthly publication – *The Log* – and this occasionally contained articles highlighting the nature of the problems. Statements were made to the press where it was thought warranted. Channels were opened with politicians to see if they would help.

Barry Sheerman, MP for Huddersfield, had formed the Parliamentary Council For Transport Safety (PACTS). I had first met him at university, where he was a lecturer in American government. I re-connected with him in the 1980s, and was invited to join PACTS. Barry and the Council provided a platform for these issues to be discussed, considered, and occasionally raised more directly with other interested politicians, and even questions to the Minister of Transport in the House of Commons, Paul Channon MP.

Barry Sheerman and I were interviewed by the BBC for a 'File on Four' edition on North Sea helicopter safety. The edition was entitled 'Regulation By Accident.' This made the point that progress on regulation was reactive – you had to wait for an actual accident or serious incident before safety improvements would be considered. It was broadcast on BBC Radio Four. Suggestions that TV stations might be interested were quashed by BALPA – it was considered to be too powerful a medium to air matters such as this, which frankly I found puzzling.

John Prescott, a former seafarer, MP for Hull, and future Deputy Prime Minister, also took an active interest in offshore safety. Both he and his staff regularly consulted me through BALPA about helicopter operations.

One had to be very careful to avoid the accusation of disloyalty to the company. However, to get a change, it was necessary to start with a criticism that some aspect of safety was unsatisfactory, and this entailed personal risk to anyone championing it. Today, such critics are called "whistle-blowers" and protected by law. In those days there was no such protection, and I subsequently learned that my dismissal had been discussed more than once.

BALPA also started to have regular meetings with the Civil Aviation Authority (CAA) on helicopter safety. The BALPA team included the Technical Secretary Terry Staples, a former RAF Wing Commander with an impressive ability to grasp a complex brief; Captain Lou de Marco, a former RAF Search and Rescue pilot, whom I regarded as the most technically adroit of us; and myself.

The CAA inspectors were always courteous, and their comments sometimes well considered; but sometimes it felt like trying to suck treacle through a straw.

Lou de Marco was honoured with a BALPA award for his contribution to helicopter safety, and shortly afterwards transferred to the CAA as an Inspector.

Back to the front line. Another aspect of survival in the event of a ditching was the question of whether crews, and indeed passengers, should be required to wear rubberized survival suits. These were standard equipment for RAF and RN pilots who operated habitually over the sea. During my first years on the North Sea, we all flew in shirt-sleeves, despite the fact that all the evidence suggested that twenty minutes in the North Sea was enough to render you incapable of all manual dexterity, with death by hypothermia close behind. Rescue in such a short window was unlikely unless the ditching took place in daylight and uncharacteristically benign weather.

The management of British Airways Helicopters accepted the argument, but, rightly, insisted that the suits be tested to prove their effectiveness. I had just been elected as a pilot representative, so I volunteered as a guinea pig. I was dispatched, with another captain, Dave Turner, for a three-day experiment at the Institute of Naval Medicine at Seafield Park, on the south coast of England. The programme was under the supervision of a Navy doctor, a Surgeon Commander, and a team of medics. We two guinea pigs were to have electrical anodes glued all over us, and, if memory serves, a thermometer inserted where the sun don't shine. We had to swallow a pill which transmitted other information about our inner reactions to cold, to a bank of electronic equipment.

The first test was to establish an unprotected baseline, so we were clad only in our British Airways uniforms before being lowered into a tank containing water chilled down to 4 degrees Celsius, simulating the temperature of the North Sea in winter. The medics watched their instruments as we slowly descended towards hypothermia. About one-and-a half hours later, our internal temperature had dropped to a critical level, and the doctor ordered us to be pulled out. We were literally wrecked. We could not stand unaided. We could not use our hands. A medic held me up, while a second stripped me of my clothing. They then lifted me bodily into a tank of warm water to revive me. The doctor said to me "You may feel disorientated for a while." He wasn't kidding. My insides were still clutched with cold, while my skin was luxuriating in a warm bath.

Then one of the medics came up to me with a beaker, and said, "Little tot for you Sir?"

I sniffed it – it was rum!

That was a surprise because only a short while previously the Navy had famously broken a centuries old tradition, and stopped the sailors' daily tot. Not at Seafield Park apparently. He held the beaker to my lips but didn't tip it far enough. Clumsily, I raised an arm to tip it further, but I wasn't in control of my limbs, and a large sluice went gulping down my throat. It hit my insides like a tongue of fire.

The medic said, "Blimey Sir – that's Pusser's Rum! You're supposed to do sippers!" Within five minutes I was drunk, and I didn't care about much anymore. They lifted me out.

We spent time recovering in a rest area, before being taken by bus to our hotel. I slept well.

The following day, we were picked up and reported for duty, or in Navy parlance we 'turned to.' This day was to be a repeat of the first, but this time with immersion suits. One thing that did intrigue me was that before being returned to the hotel the previous day, we had been asked to record exactly what we had to eat and drink; but were also advised that, if we were accompanied, to refrain from sexual activity as it might 'distort' things. The Navy was not clear about what might get distorted. I suspected this was just another Navy wind-up, but the data gathering on the second day included food eaten, drinks drunk, time spent asleep, and whether or not sexual activity had occurred. To be honest, even if I had found myself in bed with Debbie Harry, I doubt I could have kept awake. However, out of a sense of curiosity, not because it was true, I said "Yeah sorry, I did get lucky last night." The medic froze, pen poised, and looked at me with suspicion. Then, executing a quarter turn towards the doctor, he shouted, "Scuse me Sir – this officer is turning to, having had!" The doctor called back – "That's alright Chief – put him back in anyway!"

There were big smiles all round, so my suspicions about a leg-pull got stronger. Like a newly landed trout, I was duly put back in, anodes, pill, and that damn thermometer.

And so it continued for another two days, and I came close to the end of my tether. The immersion suits did not work. It was calculated that they would delay death, but not by any significant amount of time. At least we knew. Other equipment would have to be found. As a result of the experience, I could no longer sustain any illusion that drowning in the North Sea would be a gentle shivering into sleep; it would be grim. No rescue. No rum.

The Royal Navy 'honoured' me with membership of 'The Institute of Naval Medicine Frozen Chuff Club'. My certificate portrays a penguin, standing on an ice flow, teeth chattering, and clutching its private parts to keep warm. The inscription reads:

'MANY ARE COLD BUT FEW ARE FROZEN'
'Qualifying for same by voluntarily undergoing and enduring
the chilly tortures of the infamous cold-water tank.
Given under my hand this day
Frank Golden.
Director of Hypothermic Torture.'

I retain it to this day

Piper Alpha

Helicopter crews suspected that the operation of the helideck on an offshore installation was a good indicator of how things are being run generally. Some were better than others, and I had misgivings about Piper Alpha.

I had been appointed as a fleet chief pilot with British International Helicopters. In the early hours of one morning, the bedroom phone awoke me, and Brian Lawson, our Senior Ops Officer, said,

"Can you come in quick?"

I said, "What's up Brian?"

He said, "The Piper Alpha's gone!"

I said, "What are you talking about – what do you mean GONE?"

He said, "It's blown up!"

I was in the car park at Dyce airport within 30 minutes. The place was in darkness – Brian lived further out from Dyce than I did, and he was the only one with keys. I couldn't afford to waste time, so I kicked in the door, ran into my office, stripped off and donned my immersion suit. Brian arrived, and called 'Anything you need?' I shouted back, "Yes – get me a co-pilot!"

Engineers arrived and started towing the aircraft out of the hangars. We strapped in, started up, and within another thirty minutes there was a line of S61s and Super Pumas burning and turning, waiting for Air Traffic to release us to fly. The call never came. The flare on the Piper Alpha was out of control and blazing so fiercely that no helicopter could have landed. An hour later we were told to shut down. I felt desolate. Helicopters were supposed to be the final resort, standing between life and death in serious offshore incidents – but we couldn't help them.

One hundred and sixty-seven men died horribly that night. The safety vessel, which was on station for the sole purpose of dealing with this sort of emergency, could not approach close enough for its fire-fighting jets to be effective.

The Piper Alpha was a sharp, horrendous reminder that there was a price to pay for getting oil from the seabed. Ingenuity, technical brilliance and iron discipline would be needed to keep the workers in that industry safe. One mistake could have dreadful consequences, and on that night it happened.

Industrial Matters

When I was elected as a representative, I went on to the BALPA Flight Time Limitations Committee. The government had commissioned a group, chaired originally by Group Captain Douglas Bader, ('The Bader Committee') to consider how flying duty hours for crews should be limited to avoid accidents due to fatigue.

Helicopter pilots were the most vulnerable. Fatigue is a factor of the number of sectors flown, the number of take-offs, and particularly the number of landings. Few did more of these than a North Sea helicopter pilot. We never did get a satisfactory solution; it was deemed pragmatically necessary for helicopter crews to face high numbers of sectors because of the nature of the work, but we did secure industrial agreements and flight time limits that were safer than they had been. It was an important step. Other North Sea helicopter companies did not operate under the same limitations, and their flight time demands were considered by us to be insufficiently strict.

Organised North Sea helicopter pilots were lucky in another respect – they were not short of good leaders. When I joined the company, Captain Andrew Spillane chaired the union Pilots' Council. A former army pilot, Andy was charismatic, self-confident, and brought panache to the job. The Pilot's Council under his leadership negotiated industrial agreements with the company that tied the pay-rates of British Airways helicopter pilots to those of British Airways turbo-prop pilots. This benefited all North Sea pilots, union members or not. It fixed the pay standard that had to be taken into account by other companies if they were to compete successfully for qualified helicopter crew. Andy became MD of a helicopter company, and eventually went off to breed Alpacas in France – as one does.

Captain Peter Boor was the outstanding leader on the North Sea in my time. Peter Boor was a former Fleet Air Arm pilot and operated out of aircraft carriers. He was appointed Chief Pilot with Bristow Helicopters. He was left-leaning, radical, ethically uncompromising, and fearless. Peter was instrumental in forming a company in the aftermath of the Bristow strike, and with a team of hand-picked flyers, operated out of Norway. The company was run as a pilots' co-operative and delivered a high standard of skill and reliability to the Norwegian oil industry. He eventually became Chief Pilot of British International Helicopters. He would never call himself a boss – he didn't use that kind of language – but he didn't need to. He was instinctively great with people, and I never met his like in being able to persuade others to his point of view. In 2005 he was honoured by the Royal Aeronautical Society for his contribution to operations on the North Sea.

Another former union representative was Captain Steven Stubbs. A likeable man with a deep chuckle, he had a mischievous sense of humour, and a prodigious practical intelligence. In the 1980s, when personal computing was in its infancy, Steve was appointed Chief Pilot, and almost single-handedly drove the introduction of IT into the company. I remember one of his programmes – written by himself – hanging from his office wall. It was eight feet long – and I didn't understand a word of it! He rose to become Flight Ops Director of the company.

For my money, Captain Lou de Marco was the best man technically. To fly with Lou was like having Google in the cockpit twenty years before it was thought of. His knowledge was prodigious; but that didn't guarantee a quiet life. One evening, I was in command of an aircraft outbound to an installation. Fifteen minutes ahead of me was another S61 captained by Lou. He overshot the approach to return to base because the turbulence generated by the superstructure had made landing unsafe. My co-pilot Captain Tony Buckley and I glanced at each other – we were bound for the same installation, and the same heli-deck. We were also aware that one oil company had banned a pilot from all its installations because he had done something similar and diverted. Tony said to me 'What will we do?'

I knew that if conditions had changed and I approached and landed when Lou had refused there could be consequences. Lou might be out to dry. I did not want that to happen, and for a few minutes I found myself struggling with a real dilemma. As it so happened the turbulence on our approach was violent, so we too overshot to return to base – the dilemma had solved itself – this time. Some years later, after constant reports from crew, the CAA placed prohibitions on landing when the wind was within certain sectors due to the prediction of turbulence.

Lou de Marco became an Inspector with the Civil Aviation Authority. I felt disappointed when he left, until I had my view re-framed by Mark Young, the BALPA General Secretary. He said, shortly after BALPA had given Lou an award for his contribution to flight safety:

"I can't think of a place I would rather have Lou de Marco more than in the Civil Aviation Authority!"

This was consistent with Mark Young's pragmatic approach to industrial relations. He once said to me, "I am not against successful BALPA lay officials like you going into management. I would rather negotiate with someone who has had that experience, and gained a grounding in industrial relations from us, than someone who hasn't."

So, it was not uncommon for aspiring leaders to start life as a BALPA representative before moving into management in one form or another at some time later. The Senior British Airways manager responsible for industrial relations in the helicopter company was an avuncular Yorkshireman called John Patterson. He once said to me "Us lot in management watch BALPA reps closely – and if they're any good we nick 'em. Nobody makes a better gamekeeper than a good poacher!"

John was a skilled people person and negotiator, but most memorable for his earthy philosophizing and sense of humour. My favourite memory is of him standing on a dinner table in the Aberdeen Bucksburn Holiday Inn, leading the assembled company through several verses of 'Kiss My Arse I Come From Leeds!' The waiters stood around gawping in disbelief. John became Operations Director with British Airways, and later Chief Executive of GB Airways.

Exodus

In the 1980s, the fat years started to run out for us. There had been mismanagement of the company business portfolio (too many eggs in too few contractual baskets), and voluntary redundancies were called for. The position was exacerbated by the price of a barrel of Brent Crude dropping, for instance from an average of $27.5 in 1985 to $14.4 in 1986. Both union and management agreed a re-structuring of the company, with pilot, crew, and engineering reps on the working group as well as managers. I represented the pilots. The group completed its work in under a month.

I hated the thought of undoing the industrial gains – the rostering, the pay and conditions agreements that had been so hard-won. However, Mark Young framed this work as a survival plan. His brief to me was: "I want a plan that will guarantee the survival of this company with retention of as many jobs as possible for pilots,

engineers, and administration staff.' I said, "How do I do that Mark?"
He said, "I'll leave the details to you".

"Thanks Mark!"

We had to reduce staff numbers, and the reduction felt drastic.
However, my faith in Mark Young was not disappointed. He was
working behind the scenes. British Airways (BA) offered generous
redundancy terms and many pilots took them. Still, these were serious
blows to morale. Everyone had to contemplate leaving the company,
and how they might manage that.

Some of the younger BA trained pilots were offered positions as
British Airways fixed wing pilots, of which there was a shortage.
This led to the further offer that the more experienced non-BA
trained helicopter Captains would be looked on favourably, provided
they had the appropriate licences and could pass the simulator check-
rides. Quietly, a lot of helicopter pilots started studying for fixed-
wing licences.

In August 1985, a British Airtours B737 aircraft aborted a take-off
at Manchester Airport due to an engine fire. Fifty-three passengers
and two crew perished. Summoned again to New Road Harlington,
then the Head Offices of BALPA, Mark Young told me that for Colin
Marshall, the new CEO of British Airways, this experience had been
'soul-searing'. He said that Marshall never wanted another fatality
in a BA aircraft again. Amen to that! He said that BA management
were doing operational risk assessment, and that sooner or later the
high risks associated with helicopter operations would be brought to
his notice. "Meaning?" I asked.

"Meaning they might be looking for a buyer for a helicopter
company," he replied.

It seemed to make sense. BA was readying itself for the privatization
that eventually came, slimming down, simplifying purchasing and
operations. From then on, I made this a working assumption. As time
passed it became clear that this actually was what was happening. All
sorts of strangers visited British Airways Helicopters to look us over;
and then it was declared openly. There was objection, but to no avail.

In September 1986, BAH was sold by BA to Robert Maxwell, with a new name of British International Helicopters, and a new logo –a Lion Rampant.

There are bad outcomes, and there are worse outcomes. For the staff of BIH this was the worst outcome. Not only our skills and endeavours, but our pension funds were transferred.

It was only after the death of Maxwell, five years later that we found out what he had been doing with our pension funding. All the endeavour and skill and grit that had raised those funds had been treated with utter contempt, and misappropriated. This was monstrous by any standard. Eventually after persistent effort by government and others, some of the funds were recovered, but not before a long period of anxiety for the victims.

Two months later, one of our Boeing-Vertol 234 Chinooks – G-BWFC – crashed on approach to Sumburgh airport in the Shetlands killing forty-five people. Colin Marshall's instincts had been right. It crashed with the BIH logo on it – not that of British Airways. It was cold comfort to us that a man of Colin Marshall's stature should have understood our reservations about safety so clearly.

The exodus continued, with fixed-wing airlines like Dan Air and British Airways recruiting experienced helicopter crew. One of the first was Captain Dave Chinn. He worked out the best approach to getting a commercial fixed wing flying licence for helicopter pilots. He then assisted others to follow his lead. He wrote a paper, entitled 'What to do to fly for Dan', which he distributed to friends and colleagues. One of his initial postings included the very short leg indeed from Gatwick to Lasham in Hampshire, where Dan Air had a maintenance base, in a Boeing 727 aircraft. He described it as "Taking a jet down the pub!"

British Airways posted advertisements saying "Time For a Change", inviting helicopter pilots to apply for service with them.

The exodus aggravated issues on the North Sea about safety, skill-levels, and experience. One evening I was having a quiet pint in the

Dyce Skean Dhu Hotel with Lou De Marco, now with the CAA. He said, "I worry when I talk to an oil company executive who tells me that the main part of his job is to squeeze as much out of helicopter costs as he can."

Some weeks later, I was talking with one such oil company executive, ironically himself a former helicopter pilot, who said, "I'm concerned that so much professional helicopter experience is leaving the North Sea!" It was as if he had no understanding at all that the oil companies' approach to transport economics might have something to do with that.

My personal exodus from the North Sea was via Cranfield School of Management. My interests were now completely re-focused on business management and organizational performance. So, in 1987, having been promoted into a management position, I applied to the company to sponsor me to study for a Masters degree in Business Administration (MBA). The company refused, so I got a bank loan and did it secretly by distance learning anyway. Two years later I believe I became Cranfield School of Management's first post-graduate with a covert MBA. After a year with the International Test Pilots' School, I was invited to take up a senior executive position with British Airways, firstly managing Terminal Four at Heathrow, then managing BA Operations Control, as my first two appointments.

I was no longer a helicopter captain, and I have never flown a helicopter since. To this day, I remain slightly surprised at the ease with which I gave up professional flying after all those years and flying hours at the controls of aircraft, but that is the way it happened. My interests and ambitions had changed.

I still admire helicopters and cannot resist standing and looking up every time I hear an RAF Puma or a Chinook growling overhead. They are marvellous machines, with unique capabilities. In the military they are battle winners. On the North Sea they made possible a rate of production that would not have been within reach without them and the people who crewed and engineered them.

I still feel pride at having been North Sea helicopter aircrew.

Chapter Seventeen

The Piper Alpha Disaster

Captain Graham Church

It was just another day in Paradise. The weather was benign with light winds and enough sunshine for one roughneck to take himself to the medic to treat his sunburn: the helideck on the *Tharos* did have uses other than for us to operate the morning and evening shuttles and the crew changes.

The Multi Support Vessel (MSV) *Tharos* was a semi-submersible offshore safety support vessel where we were based with a Sikorsky S76 helicopter shuttling various offshore workers to and from their daily duties. In particular, we would take the divers to locations such as the Piper and Cormorant Alpha, also owned by Occidental Petroleum. We were flying single-pilot for most trips by then, and that meant that one of the divers would be sitting in the co-pilot's seat for the short shuttle. Invariably as you became airborne there would be a gruff voice in your headset suggesting, "Alright, now scare us". Some of the trips were too short even to think up a neat reply since we were barely half a kilometre from the Piper, being moored off its west face.

The Piper Alpha platform was one of the giants of the North Sea, located 120 miles north- east of Aberdeen, standing in water almost 500 feet deep. Initially it drilled for oil and with its thirty-six wells, at its peak, was producing more oil than any other in the world. Subsequently, it also handled gas and was linked to the Claymore and Tartan platforms, a situation that would compound what eventually happened. The *Tharos* was moored close by and had occasionally linked itself to the Alpha with a bridge; the *Silver Pit* – a converted trawler- was stationed in the vicinity to offer assistance if there were a major evacuation. This formed the triangle of production and protection.

We had a dispensation from the CAA to operate long days as long as there was some definite down-time in the middle of the day. When one of the visiting Texans found that we could not fly in the middle of the day he declared that we were as bad as the scaffolders, who also had strict working hours. Actually, he put it rather more bluntly I seem to remember. The spare time most of us did have, we spent in the gym or occasionally in the cinema. When in the gym we would sometimes be joined by a particular off-duty diver. He was not a large person but was obviously strong, a facet which would be called upon later. Meanwhile, Chris Mutton, one of the pilots, hoped to make his fortune by selling a guaranteed sleeping remedy: he found that he had always nodded off by the time he reached page seven of a tome entitled *History of the World*.

Life had quietly bobbled along for some time in this way, with the occasional interesting interlude for variety. One week the winds had settled fairly consistently above 45 knots. There was a small hangar on the *Tharos* but it was for a Dauphin that could fold its main rotor blades, so being too wide our beast had to stay outside. After a couple of days blocking the deck, unable to start up and engage rotors given the strong winds, we needed to make way for an aircraft from onshore which was inbound for a crew change. There was a second area to which we could tow the aircraft, but we had to loosely lay boiler plate to cross a gap. Loading up the aircraft with 'volunteers' to give it some weight and stability, we attached a small tug and dragged the S76 off the main deck. As we were being buffeted by the cross-wind, a voice from a disgruntled rigger was heard to query why we could not use youngsters from a youth opportunity scheme instead.

Having just arrived offshore on 6 July 1988 to join Ivor Griffiths as the other pilot, I made my way to our shared cabin and had climbed into my bunk shortly before 10pm in readiness for the early shuttle in the morning. Almost straight away a loud bang disrupted the quiet hum of the semi-sub. It is not that odd to hear the occasional loud noise and even a judder run through the vessel since it is in effect a building site. Perhaps this time one of the supply boats had nudged one of the legs or a crane had placed a load more positively than usual. However, it was sufficiently different to warrant clambering out of bed to see what was happening. We went up to the helideck to check the aircraft and could immediately see a fairly small but extremely intense fire part way up the west side of the Piper Alpha.

Ivor and I jumped into the S76, Yankee Bravo, having removed, with the engineer, its nightclothes of tie-downs and engine blanks. We were cleared by the OIM to get airborne, and shortly afterwards were downwind of the Alpha looking to line ourselves up for a landing on the helipad. But in just that short time the fire had developed and with a westerly wind had blanketed the helideck in thick, choking smoke. Our task became one of sending back situation reports and using Ivor's camera to take photographs of the rapidly developing fire beneath us, for the inquiry which would undoubtedly follow.

The black smoke quickly increased in volume and started to dwarf the rig, giant that it was, cloaking the fire that was rapidly consuming the structure. The fire had swiftly taken complete control of the platform, aided by the fact that the fire had started on the west side and was being fanned across the platform by a westerly breeze. At one point Ivor thought he had seen the helideck through the smoke and once again we manoeuvred to set ourselves up on finals, but before we could consider beginning the approach it had disappeared again: it was a crushing disappointment that there was nothing we could do for those on board, many of whom we had flown over the years to and from the rigs. Some weeks later I met the Helicopter Landing Officer (HLO) who had survived the night by jumping into the sea from the helideck, and he said it was probably just as well we could not land because we would most likely not have made it airborne again.

A loose flange had allowed the escape of some condensate which probably had then been ignited by an electrostatic charge resulting in the first, intense fire. Twenty minutes later a riser from the Tartan A platform which routed through the Piper *en route* to the Flotta terminal in the Orkneys was breached by the heat and in sixty seconds released over one million cubic feet of gas which had instantly ignited. Thirty minutes later the pipe from the nearby MCP-01 was also breached and it belched a massive 51 million cubic feet of gas into the inferno. At this point the energy consumption rate was about 100 gigawatts, or three times the rate of the UK's total energy consumption but this was taking place at a single location in The North Sea, to a single community. The whole platform was, within a short time, engulfed by flames which were by then utterly uncontainable, and which were shooting hundreds of feet into the air. It was then that the heat became so intense that the Piper started melting. Huge girders and the metal skeleton were sweating themselves to death in a parody of perspiration. They were dripping into the sea as the fire melted the solid steel, plunging beads of white-hot metal into the water, ensuring that it was unlikely there would be any more survivors to collect even if they had initially escaped. As the rig was melting, it started to tilt, which resulted in the fast rescue craft being subjected to a shower of debris. The helideck adopted a 45-degree angle before eventually succumbing to gravity and, along with the accommodation module where many workers had been gathered, disappeared into the sea. The whole sky was lit up by one enormous firework, and both the sky and sea had turned orange.

Throughout, there had been a number of very brave guys from the various vessels in the vicinity who had launched fast rescue craft to try and scoop anybody out of the water who had survived either a jump from the side of the platform or a climb down its legs. Some of them paid with their lives as the heat was intense and parts of the structure detached and crashed into the sea, but many were rescued and were helped aboard the waiting vessels.

The *Tharos* was itself under attack. Whilst we continued with our situation reports, and thirty minutes after the MCP injection, the Claymore gas riser exploded and a further ten million cubic feet of gas were released. The Piper started belching giant balls of incandescent gas, which mimicked a slow-motion game of ten-pin bowling as they edged across the sea, at times towards the *Tharos* and at times towards the *Silver Pit*. The OIM of the *Tharos* had to pull back from these and from the intensity of the heat being generated by the fire generally, as well as turning its own fire monitors onto its decks to try and protect them. At least this meant we could land back on the helideck if required. It also made the deck available for a rescue Sea King which could winch survivors from some of the vessels and bring them to the intensive care facility on the *Tharos*. We finally reported over the radio that the platform was completely engulfed in flame: this was barely an hour since we had first become airborne.

Some survivors had managed to reach the *Silver Pit*. They had survived jumping into the water; they had managed to stay alive to swim to the boat; they had forced their burnt hands to haul them up the scramble ropes to reach the decks; and now the heat from the fireballs was so intense that they were once again under threat. It was time for the *Silver Pit* to move away. Except that its engine had failed and it was drifting. Thanks to one bit of good fortune it eventually drifted to a cooler area.

Later that night, with the Piper's wells still shooting burning gas into the sky but with the platform existing only on marine charts, it was decided that we would take Yankee Bravo off to another semi-sub about twenty miles away. We shut down there and they looked after us for the night, leaving the Tharos deck clear for the rescue and recovery aircraft to use. Even that far away they had been horrified by the spectacle they had observed.

Meanwhile there had been some amazing escapes. Some had jumped into the sea and swum to be rescued by Z-boats that had launched; one diver had jumped into the sea from the Alpha and swum the 500 metres to the *Tharos* where he climbed one of the legs and presented himself as a survivor; others had clambered down the legs of the Alpha to try and swim to the support vessel. The Z-boat teams had shown huge bravery by scooping survivors out of the water. One of them paid the price by becoming trapped beneath the platform where white-hot debris had probably trapped them and exploded their engine and craft.

The next morning, we returned to the *Tharos* and there began the long process of recovering bodies and flying them back to Aberdeen. A passing American naval ship offered any help it could, but all we needed were more body bags which they duly brought across with one of their helicopters. The mortuary at Aberdeen Airport was established in a hangar more normally used for parking the snow-clearing equipment, so we would request a landing from Aberdeen Tower at the Snobase. There we were quickly unloaded and once again on our way offshore. Initially there were a number of bodies found, and out of respect for the dead, it was decided that we would only fly three back at a time in the S76 to the beach: one stretched across each of the three rows of seats. The Piper was not yet dead and care was needed as occasionally a drift of smoke would blow across the deck of the *Tharos*. A couple of the shore-based aircraft would find out how threatening this was as their engines coughed on take-off, being unable to extract enough oxygen from the black stink. Fortunately, there were no major incidents from this.

But with some of the wells still burning, more in occasional short bursts than constant flames, Red Adair was flown in to deal with the problem. We took one of his team to hover alongside and just above the Alpha to assess how to shut these down. Red Adair's famous trick of jumping into digger trucks and killing burning wells by burying them would not work here. The hover did not last too long. We had taken the doors off the S76 and put Red's man on a monkey harness in case we hit turbulence and he fell out, but when he complained that the soles of his feet, hanging outside of the aircraft, were melting, he felt he had seen enough. Meanwhile, a drilling vessel had arrived and was drilling like fury to try and reach the underground wells to relieve the pressure, thereby allowing some of the burning wells, remnants of the thirty-six that had existed, to be closed off. In the event, they were beaten to it by Red's two men who sealed the wells from the end of a crane.

The *Tharos* was continuing to operate as a giant fire engine, which was one of its design features, thereby keeping the charred remains of the Piper cool. The wind was light, and the spray was constant. The skeleton still had the lean it had developed during the night and even had a little sway occasionally but appeared to be secure. There was a dive vessel alongside and they needed the S76 to visit them to collect some items. She was positioned almost alongside the Piper with her bow deck positioned into wind and could not move from that heading. I went out single pilot with a cross-deck landing which meant the tail would be towards the main part of the vessel, and so the helideck would disappear from view momentarily as I slid sideways left for the landing. The Piper was leaning towards the boat infringing the overhead just to make it a little more challenging, and as I started to cross the deck, and therefore momentarily lost sight of it, a small gust of wind took the cooling spray from the *Tharos* and dumped it onto the S76 making the landing totally blind. I landed successfully, with a newly-cleaned aircraft.

The final part of the offshore operation was lifting the modules from the seabed that held so many bodies. A few months after the disaster, the giant crane barge DB102 arrived to raise these 400ft to the surface and place them on its huge work deck before shipping them to Flotta and handing them over to the police. We were tasked to take the S76 and base ourselves for a while on its deck, but first we had to find it. Given its departure time from Rotterdam, planned speed of the vessel, and its destination, we set off to find it, calculating a critical point which, if the barge were elusive, would result in our having to cut and run to Aberdeen. After some time, thinking that we should be drawing close but still unable to see it on a fine but hazy morning, I took the helicopter down low over the sea, and sure enough a large shape, silhouetted by the rising sun, appeared on the horizon. We were soon touching down on its equally large helideck.

It had eleven storeys and going down in the lift from the helideck we thought it would be interesting to raise a panel in the roof of the lift to see the view above us as we descended to the mess deck. It immediately threw a microswitch and the lift shuddered to a halt. The next good idea was to heave the engineer through the hatch (I have no idea why he would have trusted two pilots) to see if the microswitch could be reset, but it was beneath a guarded cover and in the end we had to recover the engineer and use the emergency telephone to call the control room and explain what had happened. The operator asked who we were and when we said two pilots and an engineer, his terse reply was "I might have known".

Once on site, the divers set to separating two of the modules and fixing clamps so they could be lifted, but the Piper was not done just yet. As the lifting of the accommodation module got under way, one of the huge metal slings unfurled and snapped, resulting in the module sliding back towards the seabed. With new slings, the lift was later successfully completed. There were always hidden dangers offshore, and whilst using a drill in one area, a diver hit a major blowback which knocked him out. This was deep, saturation diving and not a place that was forgiving, much like most of the North Sea. The unconscious diver was a big guy and his buddy was smaller, but having been in the gym with him, we knew he was strong. He managed to drag the unconscious diver into the dive chamber and wrested the cracked helmet from his head, clearing the blood from his mask, and giving mouth to mouth, which helped save his life. The diver who had suffered the blowback came offshore sometime later, and proudly displayed his split helmet.

He was one of the survivors of the Piper story, but for many the whole episode had ended as paradise lost; 167 died, and many others, who survived, suffered enormous mental distress. For others of us life continued with memories filed in the part of the brain marked 'do not disturb'.

Two excellent books that cover the events in detail are: *Fire in The Night The Piper Alpha Disaster*, Stephen McGinty, 2008 and *Piper Alpha A Survivor's Story*, Ed Punchard with Syd Higgins, 1989

Chapter Eighteen

A CAA Inspector's Perspective

Captain Lou De Marco

Ijoined the RAF in October 1962 as an Operations Clerk. Commissioned as a pilot in 1964 I did my flying training then set off for Singapore to fly helicopters during the last days of the Borneo 'Confrontation'. Then followed tours as a SAR pilot, ground tours, an all too brief go on fighters and finally to the VIP Squadron at Northolt. Nearly every station I was posted to seemed to close down around me, as the RAF contracted and withdrew from the Far and Middle East, and I felt that the service had become very introspective and perhaps was trying to tell me something. When I began flying many were the excellent RAF pilots who were aviators first and only officers because they needed to be allowed to be aviators. By 1975 the RAF seemed to find it hard to cope with those pilots not wishing to grasp the greasy pole of promotion and, certainly in my case, was unable to offer the amount of flying I wanted either. So, I took 'Premature Voluntary Retirement'.

Typically, the airline industry was undergoing the bust part of one of its boom-bust cycles, so looking in the direction of aeroplane flying was less than promising. British Airways Helicopters (BAH) wanted pilots though, for its expanding North Sea operations. I went for an interview with the Flight Manager, Mike Evans, at company headquarters in the 'Beehive' at Gatwick. He was able to offer as much flying in a year as the RAF gave me in four, better pay, all the benefits of British Airways and a command on the Sikorsky S61 in six months, provided that I was suitable, and accepted Sumburgh in the Shetland Islands as my base. Before deciding, I was allowed a familiarisation trip and duly flew to Aberdeen and then on to Sumburgh in February 1976. At that point I realised just how far away Shetland is from London! When I arrived (by Viscount), I also realised why the familiarisation trip was a good idea; there were no trees for a start, and a room in temporary Portakabin accommodation at the Sumburgh Hotel. I think there was a Westerly wind of about 35 knots when I arrived, and it was grey, and very cold. The walls of the Portakabin were 'panting' in the wind, and I swear you could squint between the adjoining room dividing walls as they bulged to reveal the length of the building. This needed some thought, and a word with my then girlfriend! The BA residents seemed a cheery lot though and I subsequently discovered that my acceptance of the job would make me the seventeenth pilot on the base for the third Sikorsky S61 to be based there.

I found the training in Aberdeen exceptionally good. I remember Ground School being delivered by a former RN Chief Petty Officer named Kevin Humphries. Kevin was an excellent instructor and had an inexhaustible fund of rude stories and below deck swearwords. For part of my conversion flying training, I remember that we took an S61 helicopter, with several training captains and trainees, up to Inverness where the airfield was much quieter than Aberdeen. Aberdeen was becoming so busy by this time that training was frequently not permitted until the evening. Inverness was a much easier option and, as well as becoming familiar with the S61 I began to learn something about the complex but potentially lucrative British Airways Allowances system. For example, most hotel expenses such as food, phone and laundry could be claimed. Alcohol consumed could not. It was, however, quite easy to persuade the hotel to put 'extra vegetables' on the meal receipts. On this particular trip, I think we scored £200.00 in extra vegetables. By July 1976 I had completed my conversion course and left for Sumburgh to work as a First Officer and learn the trade. By January 1977 I had completed the Command Course and was a shiny new captain.

Learning to live in Shetland was interesting and fun. BAH allowed pilots a period in the Sumburgh Hotel whilst they endeavoured to find accommodation, whether accompanied or not. My recollection is that staying in the Sumburgh (also known as the Slumburgh) Hotel was, in itself a powerful incentive to find a house. For those with families, there was limited housing at Sumburgh and elsewhere built by the Scottish Airports and Scottish Special Housing Associations. For most folk though it was a question of trying to buy, build or rent something. In the short term I found a grass roofed stone cottage to rent at the hamlet of Scousburgh, seven miles North of Sumburgh. It was owned by crofters Willy and Emily Henderson who also ran the local shop. They and their family introduced us to the delights and traditions of Shetland and became firm friends. Shortly after, I bought and extended a modern house, also in Scousburgh. Our first child, Dorcas, was born in Lerwick hospital and delivered by Margaret Ray, whose husband Ian was the resident Loganair BN Islander pilot. Ian later became a colleague of mine at the Civil Aviation Authority, small world! So, we had our own peat banks up the hill and lived in a house overlooking the Atlantic Ocean to the West with Foula Island in the distance. It was windy when it blew though. I remember having to tie the garage roof joists to the bumper of my car to prevent the garage roof being blown off on one breezy occasion. Many cars were fitted with 'Shetland doors', which was simply a condition suffered by the vehicle when insufficient account was taken of the wind velocity and the door bent back so the hinges creased the external door skin. I remember having to tie the pram down too – all part of the joys of Shetland life!

For a passenger, travel to and from Shetland was quite easy by air but less so if moving house contents. At that time, the ship used for transport between Lerwick and Aberdeen was the St Clair. This wasn't the later swish roll on-roll-off version but a much smaller vessel. Cargo was either winched up and down from a hold on the foredeck or carried on deck on the hatches. So it was that, when we moved our household from Suffolk to Shetland, we used for the job, two 35cwt 'Luton' vans with drivers. Our two cats were installed in a van and our Scottish deerhound came as a deck passenger. The vans were tied down, outside, on the foredeck. Inevitably, it was blowing a strong gale for the journey north, and I recall seeing the first waves breaking over the bow of the ship shortly after leaving Aberdeen harbour. It became even rougher during the night and we were convinced that, by the morning, our vans (and cats) would have been swept overboard. In theory dogs were not allowed in the cabins and were to be restrained in sheltered areas on deck. That was never going to work, and we eventually recovered a very damp deerhound to our cabin, who then spent the night on the floor, legs spread-eagled against the ship's considerable movement. Our two van drivers were quite ill during the night. Morning dawned bright and clear in Lerwick and our two vans were still aboard! When they had been craned ashore, we raised the rear shutters of one, and the two cats seemed not in the least concerned about their night on the (very) high seas. The corollary to the story was that we had the van drivers as unintended guests for a couple of nights whilst we tried to move into our new abode. The inclement weather had disrupted ferry sailings and the few hotels in Lerwick were full with waiting passengers. An early lesson that one needed a good sense of humour to work in Shetland!

An apocryphal tale about the 'old' *St Clair*. Back in 1976 the rest of the UK had 625-line colour TV; not so Shetland, which made do with 405 line black and white, so the residents weren't very inclined to pay the licence fee. The story goes that those in high places decided to teach the naughty Shetlanders a lesson and despatched a TV detector van north on the *St Clair*. Whilst it was being craned off the ship at Lerwick it suffered an unfortunate mishap and was 'accidentally' dropped into the harbour. The licence detector van never visited again. Later, a colour TV aerial was installed at Bressay, a hilly island adjacent to Lerwick, so those in the immediate vicinity had colour TV. This was not much use for those of us (most of Shetland) masked from Bressay by high ground, so there began the ingenious installation of unofficial booster stations around the island. One of our pilots, John Baker, who lived nearby at Bigton, erected a mast on high ground within line of sight of Bigton and Bressay, with appropriately positioned aerials joined by a battery powered booster and, et voila, problem solved. A later addition was a wind generator to recharge the battery.

Later, the housing problem became unsustainable. BAH staff numbers had grown to 250+ at Sumburgh and Bristow also had a substantial number. Additionally, there were the support staff that could not be recruited locally. So, BAH built what it called the 'Social Club' adjacent to the airfield. This had eating, drinking, and catering facilities open to all and a number of bedrooms for what became known as the 'Aberdeen Commuters'. These pilots came to Sumburgh as needed to supplement those who were based there. They normally arrived on the first charter flight on Monday and left with the passengers they had brought from offshore on Friday. They had to present themselves for a specified flight northbound from Aberdeen but where they originated from was their choice. Several commuted from as far as the west country. When I left Sumburgh in 1980 there were 13 BAH S61s based there, supplemented by up to seven additional aircraft as required. A new passenger terminal was opened in 1979 to relieve congestion at the old prefabricated terminal adjacent to the disused runway to the north-west, but prior to that I recall once returning from offshore in my S61, to find twenty further assorted S61s, rotors turning, and waiting to load or unload at the old terminal. The passengers were flown in from elsewhere, mainly by a fleet of HS 748s chartered by the oil companies.

There could be a certain amount of enmity between the resident pilots and Aberdeen commuters, mainly to do with allowances and workload sharing, I think. It is certainly the case that, at the end of their work cycle in Shetland, the commuters were VERY keen not to miss their aircraft going South, sometimes a little too keen. It was their habit to leave their packed bags in the pilots' crew room on their last day, so they could sign in their aircraft from the flight, get swiftly changed, and away. One commuter had upset some residents on one occasion, and when he went to grab his bag and run for his trip south, he couldn't lift it because it seemed so heavy. Whilst he had been flying, someone had removed the contents, screwed the bag base to the floor and then re-packed it. Cue anger and hilarity in equal measure!

In my first few days I began to learn about the notorious Shetland weather. 'Nine months of winter, followed by three months of bad weather'. At the time, BAH and Bristow Helicopters operated from adjacent wartime hangars on the north-west side of the airport. BAH had installed portacabins inside the hangar to serve operations, engineering and admin. needs; they had also installed another portacabin outside the hangar fitted with a fridge, and the wherewithal to consume alcohol. It was known as the porta-pub.

It was an unusually fine July evening; bright sunshine, no wind or cloud and feeling genuinely warm (rare in Shetland). Assorted Bristow and BAH staff were standing outside the porta-pub discussing the day – as you do – and watching a Bristow Sikorsky S58T depart for an evening trip somewhere. There was soon a chill in the air and the far side of the airport seemed to have disappeared followed, minutes late, by the closer bits – fog had arrived, thick fog, or in Scottish doggerel, the Haar. Being new to this lark I, and some of my fellow newbies, were concerned for the welfare of the S58T. Not so the seasoned folk, who simply (and rightly) assumed that the aircraft captain had made alternative return arrangements. Flying here was going to be character-building.

I recall that at this time the three BAH S61's were 'sole use' contracted to Shell Expro (Exploration and Production). Shell demanded 24/7 availability, so pilot manning was configured at seven pilots per aircraft to meet crew duty requirements. Later, as aircraft numbers increased, the contracts varied from 'sole use' to 'ad-hoc' and were manned accordingly. Until around 1982, we were frequently stretched for pilots and overtime or 'productivity' was encouraged. Pilots would be invited to exceed the company Flight

Time Limitations scheme, up to the Civil Aviation Authority (CAA) imposed fatigue limits in exchange for these 'productivity' payments. Crews would be rostered on earlies (06-1600), days (08-1800), lates, (14-2359) or nights (22-0800) and there was also an ad-hoc search and rescue (SAR) capability built into the rosters, with the few ex-military SAR trained pilots. We also had SAR crewmen for this work, who otherwise did flight attendant, operations and safety equipment jobs.

A normal day would see the 'early' crews ready to meet the first BA Viscount, Dan Air HS748 aircraft or even Skyways DC3 Dakota from Aberdeen at around 0800. At around 0830, they would depart for the Brent oilfields or an exploration rig, about 110-120 miles north-east of Sumburgh and midway between UK and Norway. The round trip, including a rotors running passenger change and refuel offshore, would take 2 ½ -3 hours and, provided that the second load of passengers had arrived, the same crew would do another rotors running refuel/passenger change at Sumburgh before making another round trip. Total flying for this normal day would be 5-6 hours. As a quid pro quo for getting the job done as quickly as possible, rather than taking a meal break back at Sumburgh, crews were offered food and drink at the offshore destination, to be consumed on the inbound leg. This was a very variable feast! If you went to a Total (i.e. French) chartered rig, a proper, tasty meal would come up, sometimes with even a half-bottle of red wine (for later of course). Likewise, as the massive Dutch Heerema crane barges had Indonesian domestic crews, a wonderfully aromatic Indonesian dish would arrive. British rigs and platforms were rather more basic, spam (known as donkey-dick) sandwiches were common, and some crews swore that there were boot tread marks on the top from where they had been pressed together.

In those days there was no air traffic control beyond 30 nautical miles (nm) from Sumburgh to ensure separation between aircraft, so we created our own rudimentary collision avoidance techniques. Aircraft were controlled by Sumburgh within 30 nm, and between 30 and 90nm flew outbound on 'odd' radials from the Sumburgh VOR (radio) beacon, and back on the 'even' radials, spaced at 5° intervals. Flights outbound would be at 'odd' altitudes above 1000 feet(ft), and back on 'evens', vertically spaced at 500 ft. intervals. So, flights to the Brent oilfield would be out on the 055° radial at 1500 or 2500 ft., and back on the 060° radial at 1000 or 2000 ft. Below 1000ft was omnidirectional and above the Transition Level (normally 3000ft) in accordance with the Rules of the Air. Additionally, crews would make routine 'blind' radio calls every ten minutes or so, stating 30, 50, 70, or 90 miles (from Sumburgh), with altitude and estimated time for the next report. In that way we could keep a mental plot of possible conflicting traffic and listen out for anybody who might have a problem. The fun started in cold, bad weather or high winds, when all helicopters were obliged to fly at or below 1,000ft.

During winter it was common to find Atlantic low pressure systems rattling past a little north of Shetland and these led to periods of very strong West or South West winds which might exceed seventy knots (a steady 90-95 knots was the maximum I ever encountered on a flight). Such winds could lead to a groundspeed of less than fifty knots for a poor old S61 which could only make a maximum airspeed of 120 knots and might have to reduce that somewhat in the turbulence that sometimes accompanied such winds. This would double the time for the 120nm trip from the Brent Oilfield to Sumburgh, with its consequent effect on the fuel required. Flying below1,000ft and sometimes as low as 300ft could give a little relief from these headwinds.

Cold was always a problem when associated with moisture in the form of cloud, rain, hail, or snow. The S61 was cleared to fly in 'light icing' conditions, defined to mean ice accretion on a probe adjacent to the captain's side window and visible to him, of one-half inch of ice per forty air nautical miles. The probe had a graduated scale in front of it and the probe could be heated to 'burn off' an ice accumulation prior to starting a fresh assessment of accretion. Unacceptable icing was quite easy to assess without the probe though. The front windshield was heated to prevent ice accumulation, but any ice around would first form on the wiper blades. Similarly, ice and snow could be seen and felt accumulating on the flotation sponsons and struts visible from the side windows. The power required to maintain speed also increased as weight and drag caused by the ice increased. The most compelling warning of all though, was ice being shed asymmetrically by the main rotor blades. Chunks would fly off and strike the rear fuselage a mighty blow and there would be a consequent vibration through the aircraft until all the blades were clear and normality restored. Flying through convective cloud at -5 to -10° C could sometimes produce such a rapid ice build-up that leaving by the quickest means became imperative. The trouble with icing was that you could never tell how much you were going to find in the cloud until you had found it. So, flight in potential icing always needed a 'plan B'.

The other weather-related problem that existed, with icing and wind, was plain low cloud and poor visibility. Either could force helicopters to cruise as low as 250ft above the sea if in sight of it, or 500ft if not. This brought into play the weather radar as a collision avoidance and ground mapping tool, and it would be used to scan the area in front of the aircraft for possible obstructions in the shape of ships, oil rigs and the like. Amazingly, when I first arrived in Shetland, one of the aircraft had yet to be fitted with radar. In light cloud it was also possible to 'see' other helicopters in the vicinity on radar. Back in 1976 the aircraft were fitted with ancient Ecko radars drafted in from the British Airways aeroplane fleet. Later radars were better suited to the job and later still they came with pretty colour displays. There was strange anomaly concerning instrument approaches to airfields. We could fly en-route over the water at 250ft on the radar altimeter, and descend to 200ft with the destination identified, in a flight visibility of 600metres, but at Sumburgh the radar assisted approach required a cloud ceiling of 350ft over the airfield with 900metres visibility. A Decca approach required 250ft cloud ceiling. So, captains were put in the interesting position of having to make a visual approach when the weather was too bad to make an instrument approach! The

Air Traffic Control and weather limitations were changed during the 1990s and achieved rather more credibility, though the flying intensity had died down somewhat by then.

Another interesting anomaly existed offshore. Helicopter instrument approaches had been derived from those for aeroplanes without much thought for the different operating environments or circumstances. Aeroplanes descended from their cruise altitude to approach and land at an aerodrome so that's the way helicopter approaches were configured too. Consider this though; the Brent Bravo helideck, like several others subsequently, was mounted on the platform some 240ft above the sea. So there we were, making our approach using Decca (an on-board navigation aid with a moving map), the platform non-directional beacon and aircraft radar. We descended en route to a position say 5miles from the platform where we were in sight of the surface at 250ft on the radar altimeter, so we then legitimately descended to 200ft to be below cloud and obtain good(ish) visibility, with the platform in sight. However, the helideck was in cloud, though we could clearly see its outline from underneath, and maybe even its lighting through the steel safety nets surrounding it. What to do? Well, what we typically did was to slow down to the minimum speed at which we could sustain an engine failure and easily fly away (about 45 kts on the S61), brief each other on the way we would go if we lost sight of the platform and/or encountered an aircraft emergency, then gently climbed when very close to the platform, retaining sufficient visibility to land. Sometimes there would be an unintended benefit if the platform was operating its gas flare, as this would serve to 'burn off' the moisture immediately adjacent to it – frequently the helideck. It was an interpretation of the rules that became impossible later, with more stringent regulation, but it got the job done.

The Sikorsky S61 was pretty basic by present standards, but passengers loved it for its comparative roominess. I describe it more fully later. It had what was called an Automatic Flight Control System (AFCS), which was effectively a pitch, roll and heading hold. It was completely unconnected to any navigation or approach electronics, so although it would fly 'hands off 'in a straight line in the cruise, everything else was done by hand. The aircraft were fitted with conventional navigation aids but the principle offshore navigation tools were the Decca Navigator, weather radar (also used for surface vessel avoidance, rig identification and shoreline mapping), and Non Directional Beacon (NDB), in that order. Most offshore platforms and rigs were fitted with NDB's, but they were of variable use and none at all in lightning and heavy rain. The Decca was a good bit of kit for its time, but it did have idiosyncrasies. As Decca was a medium frequency hyperbolic radio chain, the lines on a chart representing the distances from the transmitters were curved. When straightened out to give a moving map presentation on a display, they distorted the geography somewhat. For instance, on a Decca Chart London appears North of Birmingham and the visible chart distance between Shetland, Orkney and Aberdeen was completely distorted. No matter, Airways and all the important routes between places were Inked onto the moving map so you just navigated along the line and learned the about idiosyncrasies.

The S61 was also an amphibian and from time to time we landed it on water. But it certainly wouldn't survive on the kind of seas normally found on the North Sea, even with the addition of inflatable flotation bags to the sponsons, as I later describe. The best hope was to be able to evacuate the aircraft before it capsized. Pilots would do 'water landings' occasionally as part of recurrent training or, more frequently, after maintenance when the hull had been breached, to check the watertight integrity. In these cases, engineers would gaffer tape the door joints around the electric and avionics bay at the nose of the aircraft to ensure that a (very) expensive mishap was avoided. Driving it around on calm water was great fun, even though the aircraft and engines needed thorough washing afterwards. At that time, BAH major helicopter maintenance was done at company headquarters at Gatwick. When necessary we would fly down to air test an aircraft after maintenance, before flying it back up to

Aberdeen or Sumburgh. These air tests sometimes required water landings, which we did in a lake a few miles east of Gatwick. I vividly recall one lovely sunny day when we swanned off to give the freshly engineered aircraft a swim. On completion of the water landings the aircraft seemed strangely reluctant to fly again. Water ingestion to the engines shouldn't have been a problem as we had avoided too much spray or splashing, and anyway it was fresh water, which, unlike seawater, does not coat the compressor blades with salt that leads to a marked reduction in performance. Eventually, we managed to drag ourselves out of the lake and returned to Gatwick. When we arrived and exited the aircraft all became clear. A large lake was forming underneath it from the drain holes situated along the hull. Someone had failed to replace the plugs. That would have been an embarrassing headline, 'helicopter sinks in Sussex lake!'

After my time with BAH I joined the Civil Aviation Authority as a Flight Operations Inspector and became a regulator, though I continued to fly on the North Sea for about a week each month to keep my hand in and an eye on what was going on. The S61s lack of sophistication meant that high levels of manual handling skill were constantly needed; there were no automatics so both pilots had to pay attention and maintain those handling skills. This was well suited to the pilots who, until the mid-1970s were almost invariably ex-military and had been used to operating in a benign military regulatory environment where personal initiative and judgement were taught and nurtured. North Sea helicopter flying was much the same at the time. From about 1977, Bristow Helicopters, which operated its own training school, began to introduce *ab-initio* co-pilots to the North Sea, and very good they were too. Similarly, British Airways found itself with a surplus of pilots newly trained at its Hamble college and so gave them the option of a quick helicopter conversion and some North Sea flying (another option was as cabin crew until demand for pilots increased!). These pilots were top quality, learned fast and bought a fresh outlook to the flight deck. Many went back to aeroplanes when BAH was sold off and went on to achieve very impressive careers as airline trainers and managers. I like to think that cutting their teeth on the North Sea burnished the latent skills they already had. From about 1985, increasingly sophisticated helicopters made inroads into the S61 fleet, but regrettably there were a number of catastrophic failures resulting in loss of life. I refer to this again later.

Looking in my logbook for 1978, I find a fax message from Total Oil Marine about a trip I did with a colleague and friend, Captain Roy Camus, on 28th November. It thanks us for doing a lot of flying for them on a crew change to the Pentagone 84 (P84) oil rig. It was certainly more flying than we would normally expect to do but reflects the need for urgency in a pioneering phase of North Sea exploration. The P84 was about one hundred and forty miles East of Orkney, and I recall that it was being de-manned of its oil exploration crew prior to a move elsewhere. When this happens, the rig is de-ballasted, the anchors are lifted and the rig is towed by tugs to the new location. It is also able to move itself a limited amount using thrusters sited at the bottom of the legs. Whether or not it was de-ballasted when we flew to it that night I can't remember, but if it was it would have presented as a fairly unstable platform to land on. A look at the weather records for the day shows a north-westerly breeze of 10-15 knots, broken cloud and normal temperature in a weak anticyclone centred on Faro. About as good as it gets at that time of year. Dusk would have been around 4.30pm.

With Roy as captain we left Sumburgh at 12.45pm, empty, for the 55-minute trip to Kirkwall on Orkney, where we collected a few passengers for the P84. The leg to the P84 would have been pleasant and quiet, away from the Sumburgh and Aberdeen traffic but with just a need to keep an ear cocked for any helicopters flying up from Aberdeen to rigs north east of Sumburgh. I expect the provision of food was of major interest to us, partly because we were going to a 'French' rig, and because it was unlikely that we would have had lunch before leaving Sumburgh. It took 55 minutes to reach Kirkwall and then a further 90 minutes to P84. A quick rotors running refuel and load up with passengers, then back to Kirkwall, the last

20 minutes after nightfall. We then swapped command and flew another night return trip between Kirkwall and P84 before the final trip from Kirkwall to P84 and thence to Aberdeen, landing at 10pm to avoid late opening charges at Aberdeen. It all added up to 9 hours 15 minutes flying without leaving the cockpit, including 4 hours 50 minutes at night but only 45 minutes instrument flying – it must have been a fine night so we just penetrated cloud on the climb and descent for each sector. After a night in the Aberdeen Skean Dhu Hotel (and doubtless a glass or two to wind down), on the next day we then did a quick trip, 3 hours 30minutes, back to Sumburgh via the Heather platform, 100nm NE of Sumburgh, followed by another quick return trip from Sumburgh to the Sea Conquest, under tow down the West side of Shetland, and back. I think I deserved my three days off after that!

Some of our pilots regularly achieved the legal limit of 9am hours flying a year and were obliged to take additional leave to avoid breaching the limit. I was always amazed, and, very proud, that we just got the job done, safely and largely with good, sometimes hilarious humour, day and night whatever the weather. Standing in Operations at Sumburgh watching S61s return in hurricane force winds, rain, snow, ice, hail and fog; day and night with no fuss and only a little excitement gave me a very warm feeling.

Gamekeeper

Why I joined? I joined the Civil Aviation Authority in September 1983. Prior to that I had flown for British Airways Helicopters (BAH) as a Training Captain, based in Sumburgh in the Shetland Islands and at Aberdeen. During 1983 British Airways was in the process of being privatised. Prime Minister Margaret Thatcher had instructed Sir John King (the recently appointed Chairman) to reduce the employee count as part of the privatisation process and had made available considerable funds to do so. This headcount reduction process seemed to be indiscriminate. Our Personal Manager used to frequently appear in Aberdeen looking for any pilot to take voluntary redundancy, even though we were short of helicopter pilots! Over a period of weeks, he presumably did not get the numbers that he was looking for, so the redundancy package offer increased as the weeks went by.

It was also becoming clear that the new regime in British Airways could see no future for the helicopter company as part of the airline, and I was aware that feelers had been put out for sale of the helicopter operation. Unsettling times.

I had joined BAH in unsettling times too. British Airways was a unionised company, and shortly after I joined, a strike took place in Bristow Helicopters, our competitor company on the North Sea. Extraordinarily (for a recently retired RAF pilot), we went on strike in support of our Bristow colleagues, who, like us were members of the pilot's union, BALPA (British Airline Pilots Association). The Bristow management of the time were vehemently anti-union. The reasons for the strike are irrelevant, but I was considerably upset by the behaviour of our British Airways mainline colleagues, who attempted to use the strike for the benefit of British Airways mainline pilots. I criticised some of this behaviour very loudly but felt that the only effective way to challenge some of the attitudes I saw, would be to become involved in the workings of the union. At the time BALPA had no helicopter technical, as opposed to industrial, representation in its organisation and so, over a period of time I became the helicopter voice on the BALPA Technical Committee and eventually formed a study group to examine helicopter matters, almost entirely concerned with burgeoning helicopter activity in support of UK oil exploration and production. Being part of the Technical Committee gave me access to BAH management, the CAA and eventually ICAO (the International Civil Aviation Organisation), to discuss safety issues concerned with North Sea helicopter operations.

My voice and face had become well known in the Operations and Airworthiness regulation parts of the CAA. I was a vocal critic of what we working pilots saw as a lack of purpose by the regulators to get to grips with regulating a demonstrably dangerous industry.

Between 1976 and 1983 helicopter activity had grown exponentially to serve UK oil exploration and we felt that safety regulation had not kept pace with it. The oil industry had a high risk, can do, culture which permeated through its contractors, helicopter operators included. BAH had a 'big airline' culture to ameliorate this to some extent; its main competitor had a 'bush flying' culture that fitted better with oil exploration, and also a considerable history of oil industry contracting in the Middle East. So, two companies with differing cultures were competing in a rapidly expanding industry with little control over their operating methods. That they were as safe as they were is extraordinary in the circumstances.

One day I received a telephone call from a senior manager at the CAA. They were about to advertise two positions in the Flight Operations Inspectorate for 'Air Taxi Operations Inspectors (ATOI)', and would I be interested in applying? I did a little research, which was unpromising. If successful I would take a pay cut of about 40per cent and as an ATOI would be involved in regulating only helicopters of less than 5700kg, something of which I had no experience and excluded use of my North Sea knowledge. It was suggested that the initial appointment would not be restrictive in terms of progression or salary, so I applied. It was important for me to remember at this stage, that until a few years previously, the predecessor organisation from which the CAA was formed, the Ministry of Aviation, was part of the Civil Service, and the CAA still carried much of that structure and culture. During the selection process I was achieved some accommodation on salary but, more importantly an assurance that my North Sea experience would be utilised as I stepped through the seniority hoops.

The challenge of becoming a regulator, the hope to make a difference, the ever more generous offer from British Airways to leave, and the uncertain future for BAH persuaded me to jump ship.

The organisation

When I started with the CAA, the Operations Division was based at Aviation House, London, opposite Holborn tube station. The façade remains, though the offices behind it are long gone. Headquarters, National Air Traffic Services (NATS) and other functions were down the road in Southampton Row, except for the Airworthiness Division at Redhill in Surrey. I already knew that plans were afoot to put the Operations and Airworthiness elements together elsewhere in a single building (they eventually became Safety Regulation Group). There were several rumours and possibilities concerning the location: Cranfield in Bedfordshire was suggested for its airfield and good communications. Stansted was a hot rumour as the CAAFU (CAA Flying Unit) already had a presence there. I plumped for buying a house in North Essex, partly based on the latter, but learned eventually that Gatwick was chosen. No matter.

Commuting to Central London wasn't a barrel of laughs but was less of a problem than when we moved to Gatwick. The options were train and tube from that pearl of Essex, Braintree, or by road with a hope of parking in the limited spaces under the building. I quickly learned that, once trained, Flight Operations Inspectors (FOI) and ATOI were 'on the road' for much of the time and commuted to London only once or twice a week.

Our working methods would be considered strange in the 2020s. The building contained mainly individual offices for its workers. I was allocated to Flight Operations Two (Flt Ops 2), one of seven 'working' sections in the Flight Operations Inspectorate. My section regulated all the helicopter operators and several large and small aeroplane operators, about forty-five in all, with both aeroplane and helicopter specialist inspectors. The Inspectorate also had executive, policy, and administration functions. At the beginning I shared an office with a fellow BAH training Captain who joined with me. We had separate conference and recreation rooms and an Executive Officer (Civil Service term) and typist to administrate the section. Each section head was a Principal Flight Operations Inspector

(PFOI) and cascaded down through Senior Flight Operations Inspector (SFOI), Flight Operations Inspector (FOI) and ATOI. You're getting the bureaucratic idea, I hope? We numbered around ten in each section. In the definition of the time, any person who operated an aircraft (aeroplane, helicopter, balloon etc) carrying passengers or cargo for hire or reward, was required to hold an AOC (Air Operators Certificate). AOCs were granted by the Flight Operations Inspectorate when the Inspectorate considered that an operator was competent to conduct such flights. The main purpose of the Inspectorate was to then continuously monitor the AOC holder to ensure that he/she remained competent.

Parts of the organisation were positively antediluvian: Much of the typing – and we generated a lot – went on the night train to Edinburgh and came back on the following night. We were issued with luncheon vouchers; useful, as we saved them up for a section lunch when several inspectors happened to be around. Communication with our operators was by letter, telex, fax or telephone, urgency dependant. Communication between Inspectors was important, and a good tradition was morning coffee at 1000 each day. Whoever was in would convene to talk, joke, and pass vital and scurrilous snippets of information. Much of the life of a FOI could be isolated, covering considerable mileage in UK and sometimes abroad on inspections of assigned operators. It was important to try to ensure that we were consistent in our dealings with operators, and Inspectors 'going native', being suborned by their assigned operators, was not unknown.

My first task was to learn how to inspect, and to gain a comprehensive working knowledge of the relevant legislation, the Air Navigation Order, and a document called Civil Aviation Publication (CAP) 360, Requirements to be met by Air Operators Certificate holders. This latter document was important, and divisive with our helicopter operators. The reason was because it was framed entirely around aeroplane operations and many felt that because helicopters were different, then different requirements should apply. This was not the case. The requirements were intended to give a framework which would ensure that, if followed, the operator achieved the potential for safe operations and, in the main served well for both varieties of aircraft. Much later, in advance of the UK becoming an EU member, we created an equivalent document specifically for helicopter operators, which detailed different arrangements where these were appropriate. My early, learning, time at the CAA began to highlight for me one of the big regulatory problems on the North Sea. Individual operators had been able to persuade the CAA that because helicopters were 'different', they should enjoy greater regulatory freedoms in some areas. Three particular areas of concern that I brought with me were Flight Times Limitations (designed to prevent excessive pilot fatigue), bad weather limits for flying, and the failures to ensure that, as far as possible, helicopters were flown in accordance with the performance classification in which they were certificated. I will return to these themes. In each case the two principal North Sea operators had been granted differing limitations, considerably different from the equivalent for aeroplanes. They had been able to persuade their individual (different) Inspectors that their unique limitations were safe. Until I joined there were no CAA inspectors with recent knowledge of North Sea helicopter flying, and there were few helicopter inspectors with any civil experience at all! That is not to say that there was a lack of aviation experience or intellect; amongst others we had two distinguished Test Pilots in the section. They both knew a great deal about flying but had precious little experience of civil aviation and were probably imbued with a 'military' mentality in relation to the acceptance of risk.

A day in the life

Apart from acquiring specialist knowledge through bookwork (we had manuals devoted to the business of inspecting, of course) and other company indoctrination, most of my training was 'on the job'; accompanying an experienced inspector on his operator visits and learning by instruction and example, how he went about his business.

We did have two female inspectors then, but not in my section, so I use the masculine form.

Because of the peculiar nature of helicopter operations, particularly onshore, we had a 'Duty Helicopter Inspector' in the building each day and took it in turns to be the said person. He was needed mainly to satisfy legal provisions that required the CAA to grant Exemptions or Permissions in respect of enabling helicopters to fly over or within urban conurbations, and close to people on the ground. This was essential for much of their daily business. In granting said exemption or permission we made a judgement about third party safety based on information that the operator provided and our own knowledge. This frequently needed direct discussions with the operator and other in-house research. The Duty Inspector also fielded questions of a more general nature from operators unable to contact their 'own' inspector, out in the field. The Duty Inspector could be a busy boy, particularly in the summer. I mention this only because it was an important element of the training process and, working under the supervision of a qualified inspector, enabled the trainee to gain an appreciation of what went on in onshore commercial helicopter flying. Operators inevitably moaned about this constant need to contact the CAA but interestingly, after my time, in the slimmed down version that came with our joining to Europe, operators complain that they could never find anyone to ask advice from in the CAA.

When I completed my training, I was allocated about ten small operators to regulate. Small in this context means operators with aircraft of less than 5.7 tonnes, though they flew from one helicopter to many, of several different types. They were scattered all over the country and in one case not only throughout the country but as far as Pakistan. this company specialised in power and pipeline patrols and underslung load work as well as passenger flying. They also had a contract with the United Nations in Pakistan in support of the refugee relief following Russian activities in Afghanistan. in the late 80's there were some 5 million Afghanis camped on the Pakistan border in enormous camps and in great privation. They employed

UK licenced ex-military Pakistani pilots who were generally good fliers. They were used to mountain flying, being adjacent to the Himalaya, and flying in the hot and high conditions that created increased potential risk for helicopters. I used to fly to Pakistan twice a year to inspect the operation and to liaise with my colleagues in the Pakistan Civil Aviation Authority. It was a fascinating operation but not without some cultural issues which had to be overcome.

Power and pipeline patrols were a good contract for small operators. They were awarded by the power generators, the National Grid and the operators of fuel and gas pipelines around the country. These facilities all needed regular inspection for damage and in the case of pipelines, problems created by them being dug up. they provided regular work and a predictable income, unlike passenger charter.

What were the operators like? Some were 'one-man bands'. A wealthy owner would buy a helicopter and employ a pilot to fly it. The owner or pilot would know that they could offset the expense by chartering when the owner did not need the aircraft, but that to do so they would need an Air Operators Certificate. They would come and go with some frequency, so there was a regular flow of applicants to be certified and regulated and it was sometimes these operators who needed a disproportionate amount of attention. Some did not see why they should have to jump through regulatory hoops to sell flights that were essentially like those they undertook with their owner. They sometimes did not understand that the risk permitted was vastly different between the two. In essence, if the owner or pilot killed themselves that was rather their choice if they did not involve third parties; but it was never acceptable to subject fare paying passengers to an unnecessary level of risk. These people, and others, would sometimes refer to us as the 'Campaign Against Aviation'. Fair enough, but they would also bleat loudly following a personal loss through others' negligence, or an insurance claim against them for negligence or worse. An unfortunate side-line to an inspector's task was to assist in an investigation of an operator's activities following a public complaint or, worse, a crash or serious incident. The technical investigation would be done by the Air Accident Investigation (AAIB) branch of the Transport Department, except for frequent noise complaints dressed up as safety issues, but there might also be issues of negligence or wilful disobedience of the requirements. The CAA had an Enforcement Branch, which would decide whether the law had been broken and, if so, whether prosecution was appropriate. If so, the inspector might find himself in court as a witness.

There were a few operators who specialised in aerial filming, using a helicopter either as an 'action vehicle' e.g. the Bond films, or using a stabilised camera system on the aircraft to film activities on the ground or in the air. There were no rules to specifically cover this area of potentially high-risk activity, and I was fortunate to be able to acquire the expertise necessary to regulate this work, in which UK was a world leader. From a CAA viewpoint, the easy, and unproductive answer would have been to say 'no, it doesn't comply with the requirements', but we found a better way. It was all about assessing the risk, looking at the mitigating measures that could be taken, and then deciding whether the residual risk was reasonable in the circumstances; risk assessment before the term became fashionable and sometimes a means of evading responsibility. I cut my teeth on Treasure Hunt – remember that? And moved on to some memorable advertisements either starring helicopters or using aerial filming to make them, and several television series and films including the Bond movies. But back to 'A day in the life.....'.

We periodically tried to split operators geographically to reduce the travelling necessary, but that never really worked with the ebb and flow of applications and revocations of AOC's. It was largely left to inspectors to organise their own activities provided that the task was completed. For a week in Scotland, the cost-effective option might be to fly, hire a car, inspect one or more operations then fly back. More often it needed the 'allocated car'. Inspectors were awarded a choice of vehicles from whichever manufacturer the CAA had contracted with. There was a basic vehicle according to grade (Civil Service again) which could be upgraded at the inspector's expense to make it better. This made sense, given the high mileage that was necessary. In 1984 we changed the vehicles at 45000miles, which I managed to achieve in eighteen months at my most peripatetic.

On Monday I might travel to Coventry, make some inspections, and then stay in a hotel locally before an early morning drive to Carlisle. I would start work with my operator there in the afternoon, stay locally and spend the following day there too before driving to a hotel near Newcastle. Thursday and Friday morning would be with my Newcastle operator, with an afternoon/evening drive home. The following Monday would be in the office, writing up reports, writing to the operators that I had been with to confirm any deficiencies I had discovered, and rectification we had agreed; and attacking my 'in' tray. Then off we'd go again! It was by no means an easy life, but we had a system of DOILs (days off in lieu), which we could accumulate to relieve the pressure. Usually, it was a pleasure to be with the operators. It was important to try to develop a relationship of mutual respect, the facility to criticise constructively, and to help the operator to find a way to go about his business whilst remaining safe and legal. I was told early on that a major quality for an inspector was a good sense of smell! The ability to sense if something wasn't quite right and then to investigate to establish whether this was justified. Also, having done an inspection and before discussing it with the operator, to ask myself 'is it safe'. If the answer was yes, then any deficiencies were easily sorted, if not, then some serious action was needed.

What form did the inspections take? There were paper examinations of aircraft Technical Logs (essentially its airworthiness maintenance record completed by pilots and engineers), Flight Logs (documents compiled in flight showing position, time, fuel consumption etc), crew duty time records, weather records and other sources. We would frequently examine the activities of an aircraft or a crew over a period of time and construct a history to be able to see whether the aircraft had been operated in accordance with the Operations Manual requirements. Aah! The Operations Manual. This was a document required by all operators in which they set out how their aircraft were to be flown. It included weather limits, crew duty limits, loading and many other factors which, if complied with, would facilitate the safe operation of their aircraft. Now I need to digress…. Again!

When I joined the CAA, we aimed to achieve safety using a 'compliance culture'. Essentially, the CAA wrote the rules and if the operator obeyed them, they would be safe. Times change! The CAA, and some of the major operators, realised that as aviation expanded, the compliance culture would not achieve the necessary levels of safety. It was not that commercial flying was becoming more dangerous, it wasn't, but it was expanding so fast that maintaining the same accident rate would result in an unacceptable number of crashes. Public perception of safety is not about accident rates per thousand flying hours, but about the number of crashes creating newspaper headlines. So, with the operators we began to create a safety management culture, where operators would take on more of the responsibility for ensuring that their operations were safe, still using a framework of regulation. The CAA would do fewer inspections and more auditing. Possible semantics here but, in essence the CAA would audit the operators' system for ensuring that they were safe rather than inspecting the operation itself. It would be supplemented by occasional inspections of a particular activity as a confidence check. This was fine for major airlines that could afford a flight safety department and had a proper management structure, less so for the one-man band.

Returning to the 1980s, what other inspections did we do? There was the 'Ramp Check', essentially a spot inspection where an inspector would appear at an aerodrome, or landing site in the helicopter context. He would observe what was going on and look for overall safety issues. He would also check the aircraft and crews to ensure that the aircraft were technically safe and the crews suitably licenced. This inspection had a particular relevance to helicopters. During large public events like the British Grand Prix, Grand National, Ascot etc., a heliport would be established to serve the swathes of helicopters transporting their passengers. It was said that, during the early 1990's, for about six hours each day over a period of three days each year, the heliport created at Silverstone for the Grand Prix was the busiest airport in the world in terms of aircraft movements. Small operators also operated 'pleasure flying' activities. At weekend summer events across the country operators would give 'joy rides' to paying attendees using helicopters with two or three passenger seats. The potential for these activities to go horribly wrong was significant, so helicopter inspectors became well familiar with Steam Fairs, County Shows, and the like, instead of taking the weekend off.

There were also facilities checks, ensuring that operators had the right physical infrastructure for their business; it's true, some operations were run from the Chief Pilot's home, and that wasn't always a bad thing! But helicopters needed hangars and maintenance facilities. A barn in the middle of nowhere was by no means unknown. Importantly too, we needed to ensure that pilots were getting proper initial and recurrent training in flying skills, their operating area and even first aid and survival should it all go wrong. There was a check to assess this too.

Perhaps the most important inspection of all, and the most difficult to achieve with small operators for practical reasons, was the Flight Inspection. This is where it all came together, where an objective assessment of the safety of an operators' crews could be made. The inspector would sit alongside the pilot(s) and observe the way they operated the aircraft. It mostly gave the inspector a warm fuzzy feeling that all was well, but just occasionally a horror story was revealed and a difficult conversation followed.

Flying

One of the really good aspects of working as an FOI were the opportunities for interesting flying. All inspectors were required to fly sufficiently to hold a current licence. There were several ways of doing this: one was through an annual allocation of hours to spend flying a particular aircraft type. The allocation was sufficient for a little refresher flying and to do the mandatory six-monthly tests.

Another was through flying the aircraft operated by the CAA; to digress; when I joined there was an organisation called Civil Aviation Flying Unit (CAAFU) at Stansted airport. Its tasks were to test initial commercial licence applicants, to train and issue ratings to commercial training pilots, to regulate the training departments of AOC holders and to inspect electronic navigation aids. For the latter task it operated two instrumented HS748 turboprops. CAAFU employed Flight Operations Inspectors (Training((FO(T)I's) and Flight Examiners (FE's).. As the reader will know, aviation really is littered with acronyms, abbreviations, and mnemonics! I apologise...... anyway. Many of the staff were experienced and dedicated airline training captains, others perhaps less so. Certainly, the place had a reputation for being a rather stuffy, stratified organisation and new commercial pilots attending to be tested found it intimidating. Personally, the training and testing I received at CAAFU hands I found excellent, but the place was dreadfully inefficient. Coincident with the rest of Safety Regulation moving to Gatwick, it was broken up and absorbed into the larger organisation.

Digression finished: CAAFU also operated a Piper Navajo 350, a small twin piston engine air-taxi, and a HS125 business jet. These were used to enable inspectors to maintain currency on piston and jet aircraft respectively. Initially I was able to resurrect my aeroplane licence and, once a month or so, would team up with a colleague and mooch off in the Navajo to the near continent, sharing the flying and probably hitting the destination supermarket at lunch-time. Effective training and enjoyment rolled into one! The Navajo disappeared with CAAFU, but we continued to lease a HS125, kept at Luton. I was fortunate to be able to qualify on the 'pocket rocket' and eventually became a training captain on it, so I flew it frequently. In addition to refresher flying it was tasked with air taxi work, mainly flying National Art Traffic Services (NATS) staff and others around UK and Europe to save on commercial air fares and working time. We also did a little government VIP flying and some interesting aviation research tasks with it.

The third way of remaining in current flying practice was to 'line fly'. Inspectors could go back to being working commercial pilots for four days a month, through an unpaid (by the operator) attachment to an AOC holder. This really was the best option of the lot and, in my view, should have been compulsory. It was just enough to remain competent and to get a good insight into what was happening at the workface. Over the years I was able to maintain currency on the North Sea with British International Helicopters (BIH) – the successor company to British Airways, with British Caledonian Helicopters, and with Bristow Helicopters. This latter move was important. Because of my earlier association with BALPA, there was a residual distrust of me by some of the 'old guard' management at Bristow. I am pleased to say that through line flying we broke that down easily, and I was also able to inspect parts of the Bristow operation without problem.

I also segued into the aeroplane world to some extent; we continued to have aeroplane operators in my section and as I moved up the promotion ladder it was important to be in touch with that part of industry. As well as the CAA aircraft flying, I began line flying with a company operating night mail and freight flights throughout Europe, mainly using Beech King Air variant turboprops. That was a rapid learning curve! They employed many young pilots, at their career beginnings, flying single pilot high intensity, all-weather night flights. It was a bit the quick or the dead; you learned quickly or........ They had several accidents, though the company was well run operationally. They also ran a scheduled service to Brussels, which I flew frequently because I could get up early in the morning, fly to Southend to do the early return flight, then continue to the office at Gatwick for the day. They also flew newspapers. A regular trip I enjoyed was to Malaga. The flight departed at 2230 from Southend, full of newspapers for the English readers on the Spanish South coast. Once there I took twelve hours rest before departing for Southend via Belgium to collect Ford parts. An interesting snippet was our discovery that our newspaper cargo increased in weight during the flight. When loaded, the paper was dry, literally hot off the press, but during flight it absorbed moisture from the cabin air and gained weight. Fortunately, the fuel burn always exceeded the newspaper weight gain. Later I did transplant, ambulance and executive flying with a company at Stansted, which I thoroughly enjoyed. It was close to my home, so the company could call when they had a need and if I was suitably rested, I could respond. The King Air flights were with a 'pilot's assistant'. These were young pilots, usually working towards their commercial licences who came along to gain experience. When there were passengers aboard, the pilot's assistant would look after radio calls and the flight paperwork but would be given the opportunity to fly the aircraft on empty sectors. I met many of them subsequently when they had become working professionals, and from the pleasure with which they greeted me, I like to think that they enjoyed being with me as much as I enjoyed having them along. They certainly relieved the boredom on ambulance flights as far away as Cyprus. Transplants were fascinating; either flying the medical team to extract, collect and return with the organ, or sometimes collecting the patient for their operation. I had a lot of good feedback from those flights. On one occasion I set off, late at night, to take some corneas to Milan (Linate). I was to meet an Italian crew there who would take them on to Southern Italy. The first bit to Linate went well. Then I had to tackle Italian customs with the corneas and paperwork in the subterranean underground vastness of that airport in the middle of the night. Let me tell you it wasn't easy, and by the time I succeeded the Italian crew were nervously looking at their watches lest they run out of available duty hours. Oh, and there was the time I slept in the cells at the guardroom of an RAF station, so that I could get some rest whilst the transplant team were doing their stuff at the local hospital. I could go on!

We tried to keep at least one inspector qualified on all the aircraft types in use by AOC holders, and he/she might become the 'lead' inspector for the type, to whom others could refer with a technical question about the aircraft. I'm delighted to say that, at one stage, I managed to have a current aircraft rating on thirteen different types and was competent to operate three of them. I enjoyed my flying with the CAA, there was enough to remain interesting and insufficient for boredom to intrude. I used to manage about 200 hours a year in total.

Airworthiness

I've referred to our Airworthiness Division; in the days before amalgamation with the EU, they were responsible for ensuring that no aircraft was registered in UK until it met extensive requirements to ensure its safety. These were British Civil Airworthiness Requirements (BCAR's) which, with the US equivalent, were the benchmark standards to which aircraft were built worldwide. They also had a parallel department to ours which allocated Airworthiness Surveyors to regulate Approved Maintenance Organisations. In other words, you couldn't mend or maintain an aircraft without a Licence or Approval. In much later days, the two departments came together with the establishment of regional offices around the country, but at the time there was some ambivalence between them. I never understood this. I enjoyed working with our airworthiness colleagues, their business was much more cut-and-dried than ours, and they had much clear thinking to offer where the calculation of risk was concerned.

In some ways the Airworthiness Division task of certificating aircraft was easier than ours – aircraft are inanimate! In simple terms, certification relied on the probabilities of failure of the various components, such that any failure should result in a probability of less than 10^{-7} of loss of the aircraft. This meant that many parts were duplicated or more, e.g. engines, so that failure of one would not be catastrophic, or multiple load-paths in structures, so that a failure in one area could be supported through the others. Some called it a 'fail-safe' philosophy.

But therein lay the problem with helicopters. Somebody once called them a triumph of ingenuity over common sense. Many components in a helicopter cannot be duplicated and some critical single components cannot share load-paths. For instance, you cannot duplicate the shaft which protrudes from the gearbox at the top of the helicopter and carries the main rotor blades, nor can it be made fail-safe. Similarly, if a single rotor blade fails, the resulting out of balance forces will destroy the aircraft and occupants. Both have happened. So, the design philosophy with such components is to give them a 'safe life'. The component is carefully built to eliminate flaws and after a fixed amount of use it is removed and scrapped or overhauled. This philosophy, though the best there is, means that the probability of catastrophic failure in a helicopter is rather higher than for an equivalent aeroplane. Back in my day it was more than two orders of magnitude higher and I am not aware that it has changed. This immediately creates a potential problem when the helicopter is operating in a hostile environment. Over the North Sea is such an environment.

An example: the Sikorsky S61N was, throughout the 1970's and 80's, the workhorse for transporting passengers and high priority freight in support of North Sea oil exploration and production, and I flew it for thousands of happy hours. It was a big, roomy helicopter, with a maximum of thirty-two passenger seats plus three crew, and two large baggage holds. When I started it was configured with up to twenty-three seats but was required to carry a cabin attendant with more than nineteen. Strangely, our competitor was given an exemption to carry more than 19 without a cabin attendant (rescinded after ditchings began to increase). I was never given a rational reason why? It was not particularly high-tech or fast, but was comfortable for passengers, good to fly, would take a lot of punishment and was reliable. It was the first helicopter able to fly in icing conditions, much needed on the North Sea. It also had a boat type hull and was certificated as an amphibian. It was certified for, as I recall, operation on water with a wave height of two feet maximum. This was a ludicrous criterion. Anybody with elementary knowledge of water will know, if only through seasickness, that the more significant factor is the wavelength to height ratio, which translates into steepness. When researching through BALPA, and later in the CAA, we found that a

14:1 ratio was critical for the S61 helicopter, and was similar for others except the BV234 Chinook, which did rather better. We regularly trained in water take-offs and landings. Unfortunately, the North Sea rarely, if ever, had a wave height of two feet or less, though it was initially assumed that this amphibious capability might confer some safety benefit. In my early days both we and our passengers wore shirt sleeves to work on the flight deck, whilst flying to the rigs – mistake. A ditching in October 1977 threw all this into relief. Fortunately, the three aboard the aircraft (in short sleeves!) suffered nothing worse than hypothermia when the helicopter almost immediately capsized in big seas. It was the beginning of incremental active and passive changes to improve survivability.

Let me tell you about 'stayupability', more formally known as multi-engine performance. Aircraft with a maximum take-off weight exceeding 12500lb were required to be able to sustain an engine failure at any stage from the beginning of take-off, and either re-land safely or proceed safely to a suitable place for landing. This was performance Group A and the S61 was so certified. This was never a problem when taking off from a conventional runway, even though, inexplicably, an operator had been granted an exemption to satisfy this requirement by dumping fuel after take-off, to enable the helicopter to climb to a safe height. This exemption was also rescinded in the late 1970s. More problematic were take-off and landings at offshore oil rigs and platforms, where the location and size of the deck landing space meant that there was a risk-period where an engine failure might result in a forced landing on the water, or a collision with the structure. This was accepted as, at the time, there was no alternative that would permit commercially viable flights to take place. Eliminating the risk period would have reduced payload to a very few passengers. Over the years we managed to reduce this risk period by improving helidecks and creating innovative flying techniques. Later helicopters like the BV234 Chinook and AS332/225 family had sufficient power in each engine that failure of one was less critical, but these new types brought a fresh set of problems with their basic integrity and shape.

So, what we had were helicopters being flown outside their certification conditions, year-round, day and night, in one of the worst environments in the world. I'll come back to this.

Regulating the North Sea

When I joined the CAA, it was not long before I received words of wisdom from a member of the senior management. This was offered because of my previous incarnation as a critic of the organisation, when speaking for BALPA. I was told that it was policy to regulate the North Sea 'with a light touch'. Now I don't know how that policy was created. The CAA operated as a 'self-funding regulatory organisation' under the auspices of the Ministry of Transport, it was never, in any sense, independent; and it's Chairman was a government appointment. At the time, under the Thatcher governments, the UK was recovering from the economic horrors of the 1960s and 70s. Fundamental to that recovery was the income derived from North Sea oil and gas. I never knew whether there was any political pressure on the CAA to not slow that income in any way, which might have resulted in such a policy. Whatever, it began to change as the loss of life through helicopter crashes began to mount.

When I was flying on the North Sea, and subsequently at the CAA, I was gratified that the whole North Sea helicopter operation was as safe as it was, given the horrendous conditions it worked in. Pilots, engineers, and operators did a great job but, with the huge amount of flying, day and night, winter and summer, statistics alone meant a probable increase in mishaps. There were thirty-four Formal Reports (reports created when there are serious accidents or incidents) by the AAIB, between April 1976 and December 2016. Of those, two were Search and Rescue flights, included because they were in support of oil exploration and one involved an aircraft operating on a dedicated oil company contract. Twenty-two involved mechanical failures, of which seven were sufficiently catastrophic to be unsurvivable although, amazingly, in one case there were two survivors (BV234, 6 November 1986). Fourteen, although potentially catastrophic, resulted in forced landings or ditchings, some requiring great skill and cool thinking by the crews. One involved mechanical failure but the aircraft was not recovered, and the crew perished, so the precise cause remains unknown. There were also ten crashes, some fatal, where human factors were found to be the primary cause. Interestingly, from the eighties onwards, and until 2013, as newer, more sophisticated aircraft were introduced to the task the fatal accident rate from all causes increased rather than the expected converse, and this is what we were dealing with during my time at the CAA.

After a while, when I had served my 'apprenticeship' in the CAA, and they accepted that my horns were only used when a sharp dig was necessary, the time came to allot me a North Sea operator. British Caledonian Helicopters (B.Cal) was, at the time, taking over from British International, as the operator of the Heathrow-Gatwick shuttle service. I had previous experience of this when it was introduced by BAH, so it was given to me to look after, shortly followed by the North Sea operation. They operated the Bell 214ST amongst other types and, as we had no qualified inspectors on it, I went off to Texas to do the training course, and subsequently did my line-flying on it with B.Cal and, eventually, Bristow. I also subsequently looked after parts of British International, and even the Scottish aeroplane air ambulance operation contracted to Bond.

I have referred to the increasing number of accidents and serious incidents. During the 1980s and 90s there were Fatal Accident Enquiries, other legal examinations and several groups and committees formed to examine and improve the North Sea helicopter 'problem'. Usefully, they generally included representatives from operators, oil companies and the CAA, to improve the situation. Little could be done about the basic mechanical vulnerability of the helicopter, but we could certainly reduce the total risk, by improving the accident record in other areas. Several modifications were made, to improve the occupants' prospect of survival following an emergency landing on water. Helicopter flotation capability was improved using inflatable bags attached to the fuselage; egress through the emergency exits and the lighting of them improved, together with life rafts that could be automatically jettisoned or accessed from outside the aircraft. Eventually, led by an oil company, in-house limits were placed on flying in the worst sea conditions. Passengers, like crew, were given escape and survival training, and survival suits became the norm.

An attempt was made to reduce the probability of major mechanical failures through development of Health and Usage Monitoring Systems (HUMS). This consisted of several sensors mounted around the aircraft which would, inter alia, detect a change in frequency of revolving parts which could portend a major failure. HUMS certainly helped, but only when its data was effectively interpreted, and correct action taken. Regrettably, this was not always inevitable – the man machine interface was not always perfect. Other improvements included emergency lubrication systems for critical gearbox components and the like.

There were also human factors related accidents, the causes of which could be tackled. Crew fatigue was interesting. In the early days, British Airways Helicopters had a Crew Duty Scheme that reflected the industrial limitations agreed through collective bargaining by the Union, so crew fatigue was largely prevented. Its competitor, meanwhile, had no such arrangement, so its Scheme reflected the CAA requirements, which were intended to prevent fatigue in aeroplane operations, modified for helicopters with the agreement of its inspector. As time went by, the Schemes became common and were changed to be more suitable for the task. An example was the number of short, offshore sectors that could be flown without a break. Another considered the effects on the crew of flying long periods wearing a survival suit.

Other measures sought to reduce the risk period when taking off and landing offshore. Take- off and landing techniques were trialled which, with weights assessed according to the prevailing weather conditions and landing space obstructions. These reduced risks but did not remove them. Improvements were made to these offshore 'helidecks' to reduce take-off and landing obstructions, turbulence and the effects of hot gas flares.

Training for pilots was improved; the introduction of flight simulators being an early step. Survival training helped when it all went wrong, and new aircraft types began to automate some of the flying task. Air traffic control services offshore were implemented, which reduced the likelihood of collision and the time taken to aid a distressed helicopter, and measures were taken to reduce the administrative burden on the flight-deck caused by the need to calculate passenger and freight loads. Some of the notoriously lax operating weather limitations were improved. Some readers might remember being able to operate the S61 to category two limits on an Instrument Landing System approach, without even an autopilot. Others might remember being able to descend through cloud to 200 feet offshore, with the intention of then landing on a helideck situated, in cloud, at 240 feet.

It would be good to believe that these measures worked, and where survival of ditched occupants was concerned, they demonstrably did. Regrettably, it is not possible to quantify many of the measures. It is enough to say that, despite the improvements that were made, the fatal accident rate continued to increase for some time. It was clear that we hadn't tamed the catastrophic failure problem, some of the newer aircraft types were demonstrably less safe than their predecessors. The sophisticated automatic flight systems fitted to new types also failed to prevent pilot induced crashes. It was, and remains, a truly challenging environment.

Chapter Nineteen

An Oil Industry Perspective

Captain Chris Twyman

I knew from the age of twelve that I wanted to fly and as Concorde was just being built, I aimed high and set my heart on flying it. I built a balsa wood model of Concorde, strapped a glow-plug engine on the back and set it flying. It did, but I never saw it again as it disappeared over the horizon. I should have taken note of that because I never did fly Concorde or went as a passenger. I joined the RN/Fleet Air Arm, ostensibly to fly fixed wing off carriers but due to the then government cuts ended up on helicopters. I enjoyed my time in the RN and other than training and a time as a QHI (Qualified Helicopter Instructor) spent my front-line time flying off the back-end of frigates. Little did I know at the time that flying around at no more than 400 feet above water, much of it below 200 feet, would help me in my role of a North Sea Helicopter Pilot. After eight years in the RN it was time for a change, I gained my Commercial Pilot's Licence and wrote to a number of helicopter companies. After an interview and a visit to Shetland with my wife I decided to join British Airways Helicopters Ltd (BAHL). At that time the company were very keen to get pilots to live in Shetland and promised a command in six months if one went to live there so I accepted the job offer to be based in the Shetlands.

I joined BAHL in the August of 1977 for ground school and then departed for the Shetlands mid-September, to do the flying training for the type rating. The training was first class and after five hours on type and an initial line check I was released to the Line Trainers to carry passengers to the platforms and rigs. In the meantime, my wife and 20-month-old son moved from Redruth in Cornwall to 'sunny' Shetland. A bit of a culture shock to begin with as there was a lack of housing so we lived in a hotel room for four months until we managed to find a house to buy.

I was glad of the 6-month period as co-pilot as it enabled me to better understand the S61, company procedures, the vagaries of the Shetland weather and get used to the 2-pilot crew concept bearing in mind I had spent all my operational time in the Navy flying single pilot. The flying at this time was similar to my previous experience in the RN, Visual Meteorological Rules (VMC), which meant you had to remain in sight of the land or water and keep clear of cloud, flying mainly over water and at the end of an outbound leg landing on a large helideck which did not move, unless you were landing on a drilling rig/boat which could move in extreme weather but nothing like the helideck of a frigate! One had to guard against monotony because on the few sunny days flying at 2,000–3,000 feet it was easy for one or both pilots to fall asleep, which did happen occasionally.

At this time the Sikorsky S61 was the workhorse of the North Sea beloved of passengers and most pilots but with inherent weaknesses, in particular the main rotor gearbox and range/payload issues especially in bad weather. The main rotor gearbox would sometimes fail at the high-speed shaft input which would need a rapid descent and a landing on water. I knew of at least three such occurrences in BAH over my fourteen years on the North Sea together with a number of gearbox/engine oil leeks which led to shutdowns offshore and diversions to Unst. Fortunately, none of these occurrences led to fatalities. The other issue was the payload range of the S61 operating out of Shetland as under Visual Flight Rules (VFR) you had to have enough fuel to fly offshore and then in the event of an engine failure or deck being unavailable have fuel to divert back to a land aerodrome plus 5 per cent of the total route fuel and stipulated reserves. As long as the weather was reasonable and cloud base above 1,000 feet, wind not more than 20/30 knots then we could carry seventeen to nineteen passengers from Sumburgh with an Unst diversion which kept the oil companies (customers) happy as they always wanted maximum payload. If the weather was worse, we had to carry more fuel especially inbound to Sumburgh which meant less passengers and an unhappy customer. At this time our major customer in Shetlands was Shell with up to eight helicopters on contract especially during the construction phase. We were always under pressure from our management to increase payloads or take an extra 50/100 pounds or an extra passenger, because of direct or indirect pressure from the customer.

The first eighteen months to two years that I flew out of Sumburgh to the East Shetlands Basin we did not have instrument ratings, which I never understood as the weather was notorious for catching one out. Looking back at this I always assumed this was a combination of cost of training both in money and time of pilots away from flying the line and a fear that it would lead to reduced payloads in marginal weather! Many times, pilots were caught out by weather and ended up coming back to Sumburgh at very low level sometimes at 50 to 100 feet looking for the end of the runway. Sometimes you had no choice and even though we had no instrument ratings had to climb up into the cloud and ask Sumburgh air traffic for a Ground Controlled Approach (GCA). Thank you to the controllers who always managed to put me at the end of the runway! This happened with monotonous regularity because at that time the meteorological reporting was not very accurate and the Shetlands had a habit of producing un-forecasted fog in minutes, literally, especially in the spring, early summer and autumn. After a time and many Occurrence Reports the CAA acted and insisted that pilots obtained Instrument ratings. The other issue was that there was no Instrument Landing System (ILS) at Sumburgh at that time which did not help!

Up until about 1983 there were of thousands of workers offshore in the construction phase of the Brent's, Cormorants, Alwyn and the Ninian field together with about 8 drilling rigs and accommodation rigs. At its peak, BAH had 12 S61s on contract and together with Bristow the other major operator in Sumburgh plus all the fixed wing flights bringing in the workers led to congestion at the Sumburgh old terminal. The CAA built a new terminal which was completed in 1979 but the CAA trying to recoup the approximate £8m cost substantially raised the landing fees/passenger taxes which unfortunately had a negative effect on the oil companies and Sumburgh. In 1979 Chevron (Ninian field) pulled out of Sumburgh and started flying out of Unst and Shell started to look at other options of flying direct to the ESB. In 1981 the first Chinooks capable of carrying forty-four passengers direct from Aberdeen to the ESB started flying which had a dramatic effect on the number of S61's that Shell kept at Sumburgh gradually reducing down to 1/2. At this same time Bristow were starting to introduce the Tiger (Super Puma) to the North Sea with better payload/range capabilities than the S61 so more oil companies flew direct from Aberdeen. Due to the downturn some pilots were made redundant, others, such as myself moved to Aberdeen where there was still enough work for the S61 both at Aberdeen, Beccles for southern North Sea, the Heathrow-Gatwick airlink and China and India. So, I spent the next four years commuting between all of the options, it was where the work was and it was far more exciting than working out of Aberdeen. Not that I have anything against Aberdeen but I was beginning to get bored with the monotony of flying offshore.

In 1986 British Airways helicopters was sold by BA to Robert Maxwell and changed its name to British International (BI) and several months later the worst helicopter disaster, to date took place. On the 6 November 1986 a Chinook helicopter with 3 crew and forty-four passengers ditched approximately two miles from Sumburgh Airport on final approach with the result of forty-three Shell passengers and two crew killed. It had a profound effect on myself, all other pilots and BI staff. However, within forty-eight hours all spare pilots, myself included, with a current S61 on their licence plus two airframes were flown to Sumburgh to begin Shell's crew change operations. It took about eight days for the training department to retrain some ex-S61 pilots and the engineers to take 4 S61s out of storage and get them ready for line operations. It was an amazing effort by all concerned, at a very stressful time, and I will never forget how people pulled together to save the company. Robert Maxwell did not deserve us but that is another story.

I continued to work in Shetland, commuting, for a year then I was offered a training position, which I readily accepted, as I was beginning to get bored with the line flying and being away from home so much. It was a time of upheaval because we had lost a number of experienced helicopter pilots to fixed wing and the North Sea was starting to expand again (oil prices increasing) so there was a shortage of pilots. I spent the next four years heavily involved in flying training, which I thoroughly enjoyed and together with my first 3 years in Shetland and my 18 months in China and India were the highlights of my time in the North Sea.

In 1991 I saw an advert in Flight International for pilots to work for Brunei Shell so in September 91 I resigned from BI and joined Shell Brunei two months later to fly the beloved S61. I did this for four years and then unfortunately lost my Flying Licence due to medical reasons and surprise, surprise ended up at the beginning of 1996 working for Shell in Aberdeen as a Supervisor overseeing Shell's aircraft operations in the North Sea!

Shell Years

The following account is my personal view and is no way attributable to the views of Shell Oil company or any other oil company mentioned.

I Joined Shell at their HQ in Aberdeen in early January 1996. The first day was taken up with joiners' briefings, so I only met the aircraft department late afternoon. I knew the aircraft management team as I had met them at my interview the previous month. The rest of the staff were known to me as they were the Shell reps running the passenger operations at Aberdeen and Shetland airports when I used to travel between them in my North Sea days. I learnt that my new job was to run the operations department and oversee the Aberdeen and Shetland flying operations. However, before I could do that there were various courses lined up in the first month. These included contracts, Health and Safety and finance being the most useful. I shadowed my supervisor to contract meetings, internal meetings and continued with one-to-one meetings with various senior managers as part of the very comprehensive joining procedure. After two-three months I was deemed a capable operations supervisor and let loose to run the flight operations department. I joined this department at the time of a complete change to how Shell managed their flight operations and my job was to manage the change. Previously when I started flying in the North Sea, Shell had put in place the Air Traffic Control for the East Shetland Basin. This consisted of Viking, which did the procedural control of aircraft after handover from Sumburgh/ Unst and later Scatsta, Brent approach for control of aircraft to the Shell platforms and Brent Log, which was Shell's Logistics frequency. All these roles were stationed offshore and mainly consisted of ex Air Traffic controllers. In 1995 Shell had managed to get the National Air Traffic service to take on the Viking and Brent roles that were transferred to Aberdeen Tower and Brent Log was brought onshore and rebased at the Shell Offshore Supply base at Aberdeen docks. My first job was to manage the voluntary redundancy of some fifteen personnel followed by the rebase of Brent Log. In addition, whilst all this was going on, Shell Aberdeen (Upstream) was going through a massive change(re-organisation) supposedly to become more efficient, for this read cost saving. Aircraft, Marine, Supply and road transport departments were amalgamated into Shell Logistics. I very quickly learnt from this that Shell went through change approximately every three years and it was better to accept and embrace change and be prepared with efficiency ideas in the back pocket. For my entire time in Shell Operational Units, twenty-three years, I went through seven organisational changes and for five of them, being senior enough, my ideas were accepted and acted on.

For the next two years I had very little influence on how the contracts were managed and the Aircraft department was run. However, one area where I was listened to and my ideas generally accepted was on the operational side. When I was flying from Shetland and Aberdeen there were times when I felt real and perceived pressure from the oil companies to fly when conditions were marginal. During my first few months in the job, I was given all the Fatal Accident Reports and Sheriff reports that Shell had had over the previous 20 years. One incident stuck in my mind as regards perceived pressure and that was the Shell Cormorant Alpha Bristow Tiger crash. Armed with all the accident reports and internal Shell reviews and personnel experience of the then operations, before I left British International (BI) for Shell Brunei it was apparent to me that on the day of the accident there was pressure for Bristow to fly as BI, the main contractor at the time, had turned the afternoon flights down. I was determined that under my operations no pressure perceived or otherwise would come from Shell Operations. Instructions were given to Shell operational staff that they were not to question decisions they received from the helicopter operations staff but to discuss with me, if they were uncomfortable with the decision from the operators. Unfortunately, not all oil companies acted in this manner.

The next operational area I looked at, and ended up making significant changes to, was the passenger process from check-in at Aberdeen for fixed wing travel to Sumburgh followed by a change to a helicopter for the offshore travel and the reverse process of return to Aberdeen. I could never understand why passengers checked in at Aberdeen went through check-in and the full security process and then, when they arrived at Sumburgh they collected their bags and they did the same check-in and security process before getting on the helicopter. This exercise took at least two hours and fifteen minutes per rotation of three helicopters. By doing everything at Aberdeen including the helicopter check-in, the time came down to 1 hour and 30 minutes. We used to do three rotations of three helicopters a day, while previously the last rotation passengers regularly arrived back in Aberdeen around 8pm, now with the new process it was 5.30pm. That meant that most passengers who travelled south could have same day onward connections, whereas before most had to take the overnight train or put up in a hotel and continue their journey the following day.

Three years after joining Shell Aberdeen and another organisational change I started as the contract holder for aircraft contracts. This role worked closely with the helicopter companies and the Shell Commercial Procurement (CP) department who provided contractual support and advice. In addition, as a contract holder, you were responsible to a contract owner for delivery of the contract to ensure Shell 'got what it paid for'. Each contract had a nominated CP person to assist the Contract Holders and generally this arrangement worked very well. In downturns i.e. low oil prices, oil companies would introduce cost saving targets and Shell was no exception. However, in my time as Contract Holder we never did as others would do, demand a percentage reduction for aircraft contracts. In my latter years in Shell these cost saving targets became more acrimonious with the 'Contract police' (CP), but armed with Shell Aircraft accident statistics and the support of Shell Aircraft, all the contracts/contractors I managed were never asked for a contract reduction. The other issue we had at the time was longevity of contracts, the normal contract time was two years sometimes three and we, as many other oil companies had 90-day clauses of termination for no reason. This meant that helicopter companies ended up paying higher interest rates on loans for equipment/helicopters, which was then passed on through contract rates to the oil companies. At this time Shell started paying particular interest in 'Cost Modelling' and in 2004 tendered a contract not only to cover Aberdeen but also Shell Flight operations in southern North Sea and Holland. In addition, a full line by line cost model would be used, and the contract was potentially for seven years with a 12-month limited termination clause with the no reason clause withdrawn. What amazed me with the cost model was that the helicopter companies that tendered did not have clarity on their costs. That is all we will say on the matter except I hope they do now! This contract started in

2005 with provision for the introduction of newer helicopter types like the S92, EC 225, Aw 139 and the EC 155.

Generally, all aircraft contracts are tendered, required by EU Law, and as long as a company passed the technical criteria and an audit, the contract was then awarded on the lowest tendered price. However, this then started a negotiation with the lowest bidder with the aim to get further reductions on the bid price; sometime this worked other times it did not. I have known where some contracts were further reduced and were probably at break even or worse but this in the end is counterproductive as companies go 'bust' or cut corners. A consortium of oil companies found this out when their fixed wing provider went bust. The BAA at Aberdeen placed liens on the aircraft for non-payment of airport taxes BUT Bristow who ran the consortium had prior knowledge and arranged for an operator to have two BAE 146 jets on the tarmac at Aberdeen by 10am the following day but it cost them more to run the service than the saving they made on the contract.

Just after the Second World War, Shell set up an Aircraft Department to oversee their aircraft operations worldwide and this became Shell Aircraft International (SAI). The job of this department is to annually audit Fixed Wing/Helicopter operators that Shell uses or are likely to use, review local internal air operations and offer advice and support to Operational units. In addition, the Shell aircraft Logistics teams in the Operational Units undergo a safety audit every three to five years that checks Shell HSSE compliance along with Shell Aircraft procedures etc. Other major oil companies have similar processes. A number of these were introduced in the North Sea after the Piper Alpha inquiry by Lord Cullen which had a number of safety recommendations which led to the Offshore Safety Act 1992 and the Offshore Installations (Safety Case) Regulations 1992. It also led to the advent of the requirement for Aircraft Operators to have a Safety Case which was led by Shell but unfortunately, as Shell can do, they over complicated it for the helicopter companies.

In addition, the oil companies, the members of the then United Kingdom Offshore Operations Association (UKOOA), introduced a number of safety committees and the one for helicopter operations was the UKOOA Aircraft Committee. During its existence and with the Helicopter Safety Study Group (HSSG) it assisted with the introduction of a number of safety measures Integrated Health and Usage Management Systems (HUMS), Flight Data Management (FDM), High back seats, external life rafts, automatic deployment of hull flotation, passenger survival suits, fitted lifejackets (not pouches under the seat) and a Lifejacket/rebreather combination. Through UKOOA the members agreed to fund these safety initiatives through an agreed additional flying hour charge and this was fine in the 1980/90s and early 2000, but as EU competition rules changed nervous lawyers stopped us doing it this way and it became the responsibility of individual oil companies, a retrograde step.

The UK Regulator, Civil Aviation Authority (CAA) did mandate some improvements but the helicopter world lags behind the fixed wing world by at least fifteen to twenty years. For example, Ground Collision Avoidance Systems only started to make an appearance in helicopters in 2004/5 and Aircraft Collision Avoidance Systems in 2007/8 but they had been a requirement in Fixed Wing for the previous 20 years. In my view after some of the accidents in the 1970/80s the CAA should have been quicker off the mark and regulated what is mentioned above as well as in other areas and not leave it to oil companies and industry regulating themselves that it appeared to be at times.

I have mentioned the Cormorant Alpha crash and how it shaped my behaviour but it also had a galvanising effect on Shell to look at passenger survival after an incident. Shortly after the accident they introduced an adverse weather policy which started to restrict passengers flying in very strong winds and high sea states but it was not until over twenty years later, after another fatal accident, that the regulator finally introduced sea state limits. In addition, they initiated a 'Survival In The Sea' project which looked at passenger survival suits, thermal protection, lifejackets and underwater breathing aids. The result of this research was a passenger survival system that gave offshore passengers a better chance of escaping from an upturned helicopter in the water and then having escaped from the submerged helicopter a chance of surviving water temperatures down to 4 degrees centigrade for approximately 4 hours. At the same time Shell Aircraft started to look at helicopter certification standards compared with fixed wing which started a move in 2003 to newer types of helicopters albeit at substantially increased contract prices which was not always easy to sell internally.

Looking back, I had a great career and I was privileged to have the opportunity to do what I did. I finally retired in 2018 having been involved in the offshore helicopter industry for forty-one years and the one question I keep asking myself is why it took so long for safety improvements to be regulated in the North Sea when compared with the Fixed Wing Industry. It could not have been for money as oil companies have made billions out of the North Sea and a few hundred million pounds for safety is 'chicken feed'. No other transportation industry would have taken so long for safety improvements based on the number of fatalities that occurred in the offshore helicopter transport industry.

I can only ask, were there forces at play to keep the oil flowing?

Chapter Twenty

Reflections on the Quest for Improving Safety: Helicopter Support for the North Sea Oil & Gas Industry

Major oil and gas deposits were discovered in the sector of the North Sea in 1969 and in the British sector in 1970. Construction of the massive Ekofisk Field in Norway and the BP Forties and Shell Brent fields took place during the first half of the 1970s, with production starting 1975/1976. The race was on, to harvest these immensely valuable resources.

The helicopter support centres in Aberdeen and Stavanger experienced rapid growth, with the Sikorsky S61N being the backbone for heavy support and nearly all of the pilots and engineers were ex-Service. Arriving on the North Sea during this period, was an eye opener for the pilots, who could sometimes find themselves in a queue of a dozen or more rotors running S61Ns, waiting to drop passengers at the Sumburgh Airport (old terminal), before doubling back offshore to collect another load. Hectic to say the least.

Whenever there is a rush for rewards, be it oil, gold, diamonds, or even the South Sea Bubble of 1720, the dangers involved for those at the work face are inevitable. From a rules and legislation aspect, the sensible approach would be to set out with heightened caution, then introduce relaxations as more knowledge is gained. Human nature being what it is, this is seldom the case. Rules are usually tightened consequent to serious events and the process is called 'learning by experience'. What is really needed, if work is conducted in deep mining or suspended in a helicopter over the North Sea during the severest of winter weather, is proactive rather than reactive legislation. When the initial North Sea rush for production and rewards calmed down, North Sea pilots looked for protection in two key areas: maximum wind and maximum sea state – for normal transportation flying.

This protection was unlikely to emanate from the helicopter operators themselves, as the oil companies believed that they obtained the best rates and performance from their contractors, by rotating their work on periodic renewals (ref: CAP1145 page 47). To lose a contract such as the main support work for Shell's Brent field, would be a major blow. It would not diminish the helicopter work on offer but changing your helicopter company could take you back down to the bottom of the list and damage pension prospects. So, competition was fierce – without in any way suggesting that crews would take on any flight that they believed would endanger their passengers or themselves. To create balance between the stories of the two principal helicopter companies that operated the main Shell Brent Field contact, the following tale is of a Saturday rotation some thirty years ago.

Over the Friday night, an intense low-pressure system formed in the southern North Sea and made its way north-east, virtually following the UK/Norway median line. The centre of it was around the minimum legal limit for the barometric altimeters fitted in the S61N. So, around 940mbs – which with tightly packed isobars would mean very high winds. In an early morning discussion with Shell, it was suggested that if they sent their passengers up to Sumburgh by Viscount, but left the timing of the helicopter launch up to BIH (British International Helicopters – the former British Airways Helicopters Ltd), then we would closely monitor the progress of the depression centre (where there would be zero wind for a short period) and try to time our arrival in the Brent to coincide – but no promises. Shell has its own aviation division, underpinned by operating their own helicopter support for Brunei Shell Petroleum, for more than fifty years. Their Aberdeen office kept tight control on all Shell support flights, so this was an unusual agreement. The S61N›s launched at what was estimated to be the best moment. When about 30nms from the Brent, a Sedco Oil Rig called and the dialogue was as follows:

"Is that you flying, Skipper?"

"Yes – 30 nautical miles to go for the Brent."

"Do you know what wind I'm reading here?"

"Go on."

"102 Knots !!!"

"Thank you."

Suitably impressed, we all looked to the south and could see the rig about 40 to 50 nautical miles away, in crystal clear weather with not a cloud in the sky. What could be seen on the surface was rare – the waves flattened by the extreme wind and covered by white striations. The S61N arrivals in the Brent were about 10 to 15 minutes after the zero-wind centre, but with 25kts climbing to 35kts, ideal for the deck turn round. Some moderate turbulence when breaking through the core of the tightly packed isobars, then fine. The one mitigating factor of North Sea flying in strong winds is that once in the cruise and at 2,500ft, there is no turbulence felt, even from 50ft waves, plus there is no uplift from a water surface all at the same temperature.

Was it a sensible choice to fly that day? Probably not.

Did it give a sense of achievement? Yes. Would it have been carried out in darkness? Definitely not. No North Sea crew would do so if they were aware of 100-knot winds and could not see whatever weather was heading their way.

Lastly – was it a legal flight? Answer – Yes.

Question – *Why?*

With neither the CAA introducing legislation to limit the maximum wind speed and wave height, nor the oil companies introducing in-house rules for the same two factors, the passenger and crews in UK North Sea helicopters continued routine transportation into the 1980s with insufficient protection. A situation had been allowed to continue, where there was 'An Accident Waiting to Happen'.

Between 1986 and 1992, there were three fatal accidents involving helicopter support to the Brent Field, which finally started to bring about change.

The Chinook Accident – BIH BV234LR G-BWFC – 6 November 1986

As it was descending to land at Sumburgh on return from the Brent, the Chinook suffered a catastrophic transmission failure. The two main rotor discs collided, and the aircraft fell vertically from the sky. Of the forty-four passengers and three crew onboard, only the Commander, Captain Pushp Vaid, and one passenger, survived.

By chance, the Bristow S61n SAR helicopter had just taken off from the airport on a training sortie and was quickly on site to provide good work in picking up the two survivors. Because of the main rotor and tail rotor construction and the complex transmission chain to drive them, helicopters have always been more vulnerable than conventional fixed wing aircraft. The extra complication of two main rotors that are intermeshed added to the equation. This was a straight-forward mechanical failure of the forward section of the transmission. Puzzling, as in its wide military service the Chinook is put under heavy stress and often operated in sandy areas of the world – particularly testing in a maintenance sense. Operating for Shell, its use was mostly straight and level flying between Aberdeen, Sumburgh and the Brent Field. Confidence in the machine was lost due to this tragedy and it left North Sea operations.

The Shell Brent Spa Accident – BIH S61N G-BEWL – 25 July 1990

This accident happened on a flat calm, misty day. These conditions are rare on the North Sea but will be remembered by those who flew in areas of the world such as Nigeria or the Persian/Arabian Gulf. As an offshore deck is approached, the pilot needs to concentrate his vision downwards to control the final descent into the hover prior to landing. Keeping the aircraft level is achieved instinctively by reference to the horizon. If there is no horizon due to misty conditions, then there is the option of cross referencing the artificial horizon on the instrument panel but doing so will decrease the external scan. Although the Commander was very experienced, the AAIB report lists the four landings that he made on the Brent Spa in the previous two years. On each occasion the wind was between 20 and 30 knots – normal for the middle of the northern section of the North Sea.

The AAIB report has an aerial photograph at page 10, that was taken just six minutes after the accident. It shows the Spa with the tanker moored to it and the misty conditions are evident. The Commander flew the helicopter down the port side of the tanker until it was abreast the Spa helideck, then moved laterally to the right for landing. The AAIB report says that 'the Commander's choice of approach was inexplicable considering the number of more favourable options that were open to him but it may have been influenced by his previous experiences of approaching Brent Spa in strong wind conditions' (Conclusions: 3B (iii): page 50). One possibility not raised in the report is that whilst transiting down the port of the tanker, the Commander saw better horizon clues on that heading than in other directions. This of course is pure speculation. In any event, as the S61N was moved towards and over the deck, the HLO and other witnesses considered it to be higher than normal, which would reduce visual clues. Spatial orientation was lost and the helicopter drifted rearwards until the tail rotor struck the crane superstructure. Out of control, it crashed onto the edge of the Spa deck, then fell into the sea and sank. Four passengers and the crew did not escape from the fuselage and perished. The seven passengers who escaped to the surface were quickly picked up. There were serious injuries.

This accident triggered follow up action by the CAA and helicopter operators, to try and achieve standardisation in deck operations – particularly the approach and landing phase. Not an easy task when every installation has its own individual set of factors by way of obstructions, flare plumes, turbine outlets etc. The revised legislation and guidance was entered into helicopter companies' operation manuals for all helicopter types, subsequently.

The Shell Cormorant Alpha – Bristow Super Puma G-TIGH – 14 March 1992

From 11 March 1992, an intense low pressure weather system dominated the northern section of the North Sea, sometimes referred to as a 'Polar Low'. All pilots who flew out of Sumburgh during this period will have experienced the severity of the conditions. The Shell flying programme from Monday to Friday consisted of three fixed wing transfers from Aberdeen to Sumburgh, then onwards to the East Shetland Basin by helicopter. This continual flow of helicopter rotations gave the crews the possibility to pass any weather changes to one another *en-route*. A single flight would not have that situation. The weather had been so bad at the end of Friday 13th, that it seemed quite likely that the small Saturday programme would be cancelled. Instead, early on Saturday morning, Shell called both of its contracted operators (British International Helicopters and Bristows Helicopters Ltd) looking for extra support. The fixed wing support aircraft (a BAE Viscount) was sent up to Sumburgh and BIH flew out to the East Shetland Basin with the normal crew change passengers. One of the S61N crews was asked to carry out the morning in-field shuttles, as the Bell 212 stationed on the Safe Gothia was unable to start its rotors due to the strength of the wind. After the shuttling was complete, the in-field Shell Controller asked the crew if they could remain in the field for more shuttling later on. Having experienced gusts up to 70 knots and temperatures down to -3 degrees, they responded that they thought that night shuttling may be problematic and that if they flew a further extended trip, then their flying hour availability for the Monday programme would be reduced. Eventually, Brent Traffic Radio came back to say that an outbound Puma would pick up the extra flying and that they could return to Sumburgh. By the time the crew arrived at base, they had flown over five hours.

Page 79 of the AAIB report (online) for the accident makes for daunting reading. It paints a picture of a crew doing their very best to meet the wishes of the client, under the most testing of circumstances. All North Sea pilots will have experienced those bad weather days, when the task seems to grow as the flight proceeds. G-TIGH needed a test flight at Sumburgh, post maintenance. The crew completed the flight at midday and Shell were informed that the aircraft was serviceable and ready for flight. The first task was to deliver freight to the Brent Alpha. However, the freight did not arrive in Sumburgh until 2.20pm and loading it, which required seat removal, took the time through to 3.25pm. A heavy snow squall then passed over the airfield, making it necessary to remove snow from the helicopter. Further tasking was received, entailing picking up spares from Unst for one of the two BHL Bell 212 helicopters hangered on the Safe Gothia in the Brent field. G-TIGH eventually departed Sumburgh at 4.04pm – considerably later than might have been expected. Arrival at the Brent Charley was at 5.19pm, where the freight was offloaded; thence to Safe Gothia, where BHL engineers attempted seat refitting, but it could not be managed on either this or a subsequent landing. This added to the sectors required and turning round the helicopter in extreme wind conditions was causing problems. The Commander needed a comfort visit, but it was too difficult to open the cockpit doors against the wind. Tasking in the Brent Field complete, G-TIGH departed the Brent Charley at 7.24pm. That six sectors in the Brent Field had taken 2 hours and 5 minutes, of which only 22 minutes was flight time, is testament to the extreme weather conditions and the extra complications mentioned. Those who remember working in the Brent will recall that six sectors might be accomplished in half the time taken by G-TIGH, given daylight and reasonable weather.

G-TIGH landed at Cormorant Alpha at 7.41pm and lifted at 7.48pm with fifteen passengers for the nearby Safe Supporter. Shortly after take-off, the helicopter crashed into the sea, inverted and then sank. Five passengers did not escape the fuselage and perished. Ten passengers and the crew managed to exit the helicopter and reach the surface. The only support was one of G-TIGH's dinghies which was damaged and only partially inflated but did offer a hand hold to those who reached it.

Gradually, the potential rescuers arrived on the scene. No surface vessel was close at hand as the 'Seaboard Support' had not been pre-warned of the helicopter's arrival to shuttle.

Gradually, at least four vessels arrived on location. Then three SAR helicopters: firstly, the Bristow Bell 212 from the Safe Gothia; next was a Norwegian Bell 214 from the Statfjord Oil Field, quite close by; lastly, the Bristow SAR S61N from Sumburgh.

To have all of those assets in a small area, with waves of 40ft and shrieking wind, is as challenging as it can be. Astonishingly, all twelve people in the water were recovered, although, sadly, six of them did not survive.

There were heroics involved – first and foremost, Knut Rogne, a Nowegian seamen on the Edda Fram, who with his team, recovered one survivor. Then when a second person could not be brought aboard, Knut went over the side with just a rope tied around his waist. Unsuccessful the first time, he dived in a second time and completed the recovery. Sadly, this was not a survivor. When he gave evidence at the Fatal Accident Inquiry held by Sheriff Jessop in Aberdeen, he was very understated, but others described his actions. When he left the stand, the whole court stood to applaud him and the widow of his second rescue attempt, stepped forward to shake his hand. Also, in the heroic category must come those who went down on a helicopter winch line to make recoveries. The dangers in this were highlighted when the first man down from the Bell 212, was struck in the head by the gas bottle in the damaged dinghy. Both he and Knut Rogne might have been additional fatalities that night.

Amongst those whose actions were above and beyond 'the call of duty', would fall all of the crews of the three SAR helicopters and the maritime vessels, whose expertise and actions achieved the 100 per cent recovery of those on the surface. A remarkable feat of skill and determination. One last mention is for the BIH S61N crew of Anthony Bull and Ian Mcdill, who volunteered to fly out and pick up the six survivors. Anthony had already carried out the 5 hr+ flight previously in the day. They flew back out into the stormy night and collected people who badly needed attention for injuries and hypothermia, carrying them to the Clickimin Centre landing site at Lerwick for onward transportation to the Gilbert Bain Hospital. This flight began before midnight and finished in the early hours.

There were two official publications following this tragedy.

The Aberdeen Fatal Accident Inquiry at the City Courtroom, during which Sheriff Jessop stated 'There is no reason why the flight should not have been carried out with reference to the weather conditions'.

The AAIB report states at 3. Conclusions (a) (vi) (page 66):'Weather conditions, including the sea state, at the time of this accident were severe but not outside the permitted operating envelope of the helicopter'.

The reason for these pronouncements is that, as previously suggested, the regulations of the land and the in-house rules of the oil companies, provided insufficient protection for the passengers and crews of UK North Sea commercial helicopters.

There is no doubt about this, as subsequent to this accident:

(1) Shell UK conducted a comprehensive review of their helicopter operations, which introduced a wide range of measures, including a cap on maximum sea-state and a maximum wind-speed for normal helicopter operations. As Shell were the major helicopter user in the UK sector at that time, most of the other Oil Companies followed their lead.

(2) The CAA published CAP 1145, which at Page 36 (of 293); 9.17 (a) states:- "With effect from 01 June 2014, all offshore operations are to be prohibited when the sea conditions at the

intended offshore location which the helicopter is operating
to/from exceed sea state 6".

The G-TIGH accident caused a very turbulent period for Shell UK
Aviation division right through to senior executive management. The
three helicopter accidents detailed above brought with them a loss
of life of sixty souls. Whilst the Chinook and Brent Spa accidents
were not attributable to Shell in any way, the G-TIGH tragedy was
a major problem. The question has never been asked in a Court
litigation setting – how did an oil company with a helicopter division
containing some high-calibre staff, end up chasing its two contracted
helicopter operators to carry out routine transportation in such
appalling conditions?

Being caught out by unexpected bad weather is always a possibility.
On the 15 October 1987, BIH were serving a four- month contract
with two S61s in support of the original Helikopter Service AS
of Norway. On that morning, a group of helicopters were heading
south-west from Stavanger, towards the Ekofisk and other adjacent
oil fields, when airborne discussions revealed that everybody was
entering the hover at 2500ft whilst their ASIs (air-speed indicators)
were showing normal cruise air-speed. We had flown straight into
the teeth of a hurricane which had literally stopped us in our tracks!
We all turned around and headed back to Stavanger with a tail wind
of such strength that wheels needed to be lowered with over twenty
miles still to go. It was the day that made the Met-Man, Michael
Fish, famous. A fearsome cell within a large weather system remained
undetected until it flattened most of the large trees in south-east
England and killed nineteen people.

The weather from the 11 March 1992 through and beyond the
G-TIGH accident on the 14th was completely different. It consisted
of a massive Arctic Polar Low, with its centre over northern Norway,
which became a blocked feature. Most pilots working out of
Sumburgh that week believed it was the worst spell that they had
encountered. The cloud base was low – variable but often around

500ft. There were freezing temperatures and waves of turbulent squalls, with horizontal sleet in the high winds. Some online and book-based observers thought it to be the worst weather for six years, some say since North Sea records began. The latter feels closer to the truth. There is NO doubt that the sea state during those days was 9/10/11 on the modern Beaufort Scale, varying between those three figures as squalls passed through. An online check will show the difference between the 9,10, 11 sea state range and Sea State 6 which is now the maximum.

At the time that the G-TIGH crew were talking to the Cormorant Alpha and Safe Supporter Helicopter Landing Officers (HLOs), communications were becoming difficult and confused due to the wind screeching into exposed microphones. When the rescue attempts were underway, the captains of the marine vessels were not prepared to launch their FRCs (fast rescue craft) due to the mountainous seas, which took away the possibility of low-level approach to those in the water as opposed to the high sides of the main vessel. All this from an oil company that had an adverse weather policy that stated:'No helicopter flying will take place when the sea state is such that rescues would be hampered. This is measured using a combination of wind speed and wave height'.

So, no finite parameters, but good intent. Why was it abandoned on the 14th of March?

From the time that the circumstances had been discussed, Shell's policy seemed to be that litigation proceedings must be avoided, because of the wave of adverse publicity that it might bring and its possible consequential effect on reputation, financial standing, share price etc. They had reasons for optimism as it is very difficult for trade unions to be able to muster the funds to match powerful organisations when court proceedings are sought for compensation.

There is a very informative book, named 'Paying for the Piper' – Capital and Labour in Britain's Offshore Oil Industry. Co-authored by Woolfson, Foster and Beck, it follows the path of the relatives of those who died in the G-TIGH accident, as they seek redress.

Some of the tactics described are eye-watering. Shell fought against a case being held, every inch of the way, but finally were faced by the possibility of proceedings being held by a certain Judge Caldwell in Brazoria County, Texas. 'Shell proposed an out-of-court settlement, which was reached in early 1996, nearly four years after the disaster. While the families received substantially greater compensation than they would have obtained in the British courts, the imposition of "gagging clauses" left unanswered vital questions about corporate culpability', (ref: *Paying for the Piper*, page 423).

As to the Regulator, the interface between the CAA and live offshore helicopter operations seemed very tenuous in the 1970s and 80s. The late Captain Alistair C. Gordon, Operations Manager for Bristow Helicopters, who many would regard as the most talented pilot/technician/administrator in UK commercial helicopter operations during the last forty years of the last century, passed the following observation:

'The Regulators: If I have one criticism of the CAA it is that it is getting more remote from the industry's need to grow and develop. All the bad weather work has been wasted. All the early low visibility approach minima and the offshore rig detection ranges were withdrawn in 1986 and have never been replaced.

I do not consider that many of the CAA airworthiness test pilots are competent in the operational use of helicopters. They should not be involved in the simulation of bad weather operations, which are entirely to do with the use of the aircraft, until they are competent and experienced in that area themselves. It is a fact that in the mid-80s a CAA test pilot flying as co-pilot in the Super Puma said, "I didn't realise that helicopters could operate in weather like this" (Gordon 1992:11)'. (Ref: *Paying for the Piper*: page 424). If the late Captin was still with us today, no doubt he would acknowledge that his concerns have been progressively addressed by some of the very best North Sea experienced pilots joining the Authority.

Down the years, the CAA have at times distanced themselves from North Sea operations by pointing to the fact that as an area of non-scheduled flying, then many aspects do not fall within their jurisdiction – such as offshore landing sites. Surely that just means that the regulations are from a bygone age and need updating. With offshore production well past its peak and with the cuts in the trade following the oil price crash of 2014, nevertheless the most recent surveys say that the annual number of passengers going to work offshore is around two million, with 25 per cent of them travelling through Aberdeen. For many decades, North Sea commercial helicopters have been the largest area of heavy IFR civilian helicopter activity in the world. Aberdeen Airport is still the world's largest hub for civilian helicopter flights. North Sea helicopters have played an integral part in the process of offshore oil production, which has resulted in the UK and Norway each recovering more than 40 billion barrels of oil since 1975. Nevertheless, our Regulator has sometimes seemed to suggest that they have more jurisdiction over a twin engine aircraft making a weekly scheduled run to a small Scottish island, thus highlighting that unless regulations are updated to reflect the circumstances of today, they really can look quite bizarre. To switch to a positive note, CAP 1145 published in 2014 indicates real signs of progress in these areas, and that will be applauded.

Having travelled full circle in this discussion, time to summarise:

The case has been made that in trades where there is a degree of risk involved, then those at the work face will always look to the regulators or those that control the allocation of work, to provide proactive safeguards. If either Shell UK or the CAA had introduced the measures set out in Items 1) and 2) above, prior to 14 March 1992, then Shell would not have requested the flight that G-TIGH carried out, or if they had made the request in error, then the crew would have politely declined. Eleven lives would not have been lost with all the attendant grief for families and friends. As is also the case with the six survivors who will have experienced deep trauma from the event, that may have changed their lives significantly.

Glossary of Terms

AAIB: Air Accident Investigation Branch – department tasked with investigating the causes of civil air accidents and serious incidents and making recommendations as to future prevention.

ADI: Attitude Direction Indicators – the "Master Instrument", supplying the pilot with continuous information about the aircraft's pitch and bank situation relative to the horizon

AFCS: Automatic Flight Control Unit

AS 332L: the Aerospatiale Super Puma, an up-rated long-range version of the AS330 Puma and modified for offshore work

ATC: Air traffic control

AUTOGIRO: a rotorcraft where the rotor is not powered but free spinning and backward tilting; the propellor pulls the aircraft forward and the airflow through the rotor spins it, developing the lift required.

BAHL: British Airways Helicopters Ltd

BEAUFORT SCALE: a scale for describing wind intensity based on observed sea conditions.

BV 234LR: Boeing Vertol 234 Long Range – a long range civilian version of the Chinook modified for offshore work and operated by British Airways Helicopters Ltd.

CAA: Civil Aviation Authority – the regulatory body responsible for flying standards and procedures

CGI: Computer Generated Image

Collective lever: a pilot operated lever which increases the pitch and therefore the total lift/thrust generated by the rotor blades

CPI: Crash Position Indicator – a beacon released from a helicopter on impact indicating its position

CVR: Cockpit Voice Recorder – a device for recording all pilot conversation and radio transmissions during a flight. If it can capture other critical data such as engine and gearbox parameters, fuselage and component vibration levels, this would make it a Flight Data Recorder (FDR), commonly known as a "Black Box".

DATA LINK: a network connecting one station to another for the purpose of transmitting and receiving digital information.

DESIGN AUTHORITY: delegated permission from the CAA to develop a new procedure or equipment; ultimately to be approved or rejected by the CAA

DISK AREA: the area directly below the rotating blades of a helicopter

ESB: East Shetland Basin – the major oil producing area northeast of the Shetland Islands

F-111: a supersonic multi-roll combat aircraft built by US aerospace firm General Dynamics, with an ability to alter the sweep of its wings to optimize performance at both high and low speed flight.

FIXED WING: an aircraft where the wings are fixed at one sweep angle.

FTO: Flight Technical Officer

GPS: Global Positioning System – a satellite – based navigation system

GROUND CUSHION: the cushion of high pressure air that builds up beneath a helicopter when hovering close to the ground

GUNSHIP: a heavily armed ground attack helicopter

HAAR: term for a sea fog that can reduce visibility below operating minima at coastal airfields

HDD: Head Down Display (of cockpit instruments)

HF: High frequency radio telegraphy; a long-range form of radio communication

HLO: Helicopter Deck Landing Officer

HUD: Head Up Display – projection of the instruments up on to the windscreen so the pilot can see both the external environment and the instruments without looking down directly at them.

IFR: Instrument Flight Rules-rules relating to the conduct of flights in poor weather

ILS: Instrument Landing System, equipment that can determine the aircraft's line-up relative to the glide-path and centre-line of the runway in use enabling a "blind" approach to be made

IMC: Instrument Meteorological Conditions – weather conditions in which flights must be conducted in accordance with Instrument Flight Rules (q.v.)

JUMP-JET: a jet-propelled warplane capable of vertical take-off and landing e.g. the Hawker-Siddeley Harrier

LTC: Line-training Captain

MASH: Mobile Army Surgical Hospital; a fictitious Mash operating during the Korean War (1950 – 53) was the setting for a popular film and a long running TV series.

MAYDAY CALL: international distress call indicating a life-threatening emergency, generally used by aviators and mariners; derived from the French "M'aidez!" meaning "Help me!"

MEDIVAC: medical evacuation flights

NDB: Non-Directional Beacon – a radio beacon, which enables its position to be determined relative an aircraft when the radio compass is tuned to the beacon frequency

PA: Public Address System

PITCH: the angle between the chord of a blade and the plane of rotation

PITCH: the movement of an aircraft around its lateral axis (nose up or nose down)

PSP: Personal Survival Pack; apart from the parachute it might contain a dinghy and other survival aids

QFI: Qualified Flying Instructor

QHI: Qualified Helicopter Instructor

RNAV: Area Navigation (System) – a navigation system able to use both Decca and VOR signals to calculate position. It could revert to dead reckoning if radio signals failed or were otherwise unavailable.

ROLL: the movement of an aircraft around its longitudinal axis (in some cases referred to as "bank")

ROTATIONAL VELOCITY: the rate of turn in a rotating body; in helicopters usually expressed in revolutions per minute or "RPM"

SAR: Search and Rescue

SARBE: Search and Rescue Beacon Equipment – a small powerful emergency transmitter enabling rescue helicopters and lifeboats to home onto a survivor.

SIX AXIS: a simulator capable of simulating aircraft movements around the lateral axis (pitch), the longitudinal axis (roll) and the vertical axis (yaw).

STOL: Short take-off and landing capability

STOVL: Short take-off and vertical landing capability

SWING WING: jargon for an aircraft capable of changing the angle of sweep of its wings to optimize its performance in high and low-speed flight e.g. the BAC Tornado and the General Dynamics F-111.

TP: Test pilot

TORQUE: the twisting force applied to a driveshaft

TSR2: a strike and reconnaissance aircraft developed by the British Aircraft Corporation and cancelled by the British Government

VARIABLE GEOMETRY: technical term for "swing-wing" (q.v.)

VFR: Visual Flight Rules – Rules governing the conduct of visual flight

VMC: Visual Meteorological Conditions permitting flight in accordance with Visual Flight Rules (q.v.)

VHF: Very high frequency radio band – short range radio communication

VOR: VHF Omni-directional Range – a radio navigation system enabling aircraft to track to and from a beacon on a selected radial

VTOL: vertical take-off and landing capability

YAW: the movement of an aircraft around its vertical axis (nose left or nose right)

BUSINESS TO BE DONE

We're helicopter pilots,
And things are going bad;
The flares are always on the deck
The maths are off a tad;
The wind produces turbulence,
Controller's sounding glum;
But we're helicopter pilots
And there's business to be done.

We're helicopter pilots,
And the maths are quite intense;
Intense enough to blight ourselves
From downright common sense.
But roaring rotors, runway lights,
When we take off and run
No going back, into the black
There's business to be done.

We're helicopter pilots
Airborne in a storm
The ship has foundered and capsized
Her decks are smashed and torn
There's drowning sailors in the sea
There's little time to run;
We're helicopter pilots,
And there's business to be done.

We're helicopter pilots
We never make a fuss;
Desert, mountain, ocean-wide;
It's all the same to us.
So when you feel the peril
And you think your time has run -
Listen for the chopper;
You're our business to be done.

Anon

Index